AF416918

Postscripts From Past Lives

Edited by Daniel W. Wright
and Jason Ryberg

Spartan Press

Spartan Press

Kansas City, Missouri
spartanpresskc.com

Copyright © Jason Ryberg, 2026
First Edition: 1 3 5 7 9 10 8 6 4 2
ISBN: 979-8-89975-037-3
LCCN: 2026938237

Author photos: Hank Wiseman, Sonya McGowin,
    Heather Kays, Chris Johnson

Acknowledgments:

Special thanks to Dunaway Books, the Osage Arts Community, Mark McClane and Tony Hayden.

The authors would like to thank the editors of the following publications where some of these poems (in one form or another) were formerly published:

Heather Kays: "Cityquake:" *The Literary Underground.*

Table of Contents:

Introduction:

For eleven years I have had the peculiar privilege of putting every last one of these poets in front of an audience. That sentence makes it sound organized. It's rarely been that easy.

What it actually looked like was borrowed rooms, me feeling like Kermit the Frog as I did my best to hold things together, too much money spent on liquor in hopes of luring the unfamiliar in, bartenders pretending to listen, and a small congregation of the faithful gathered to hear language do what it has always done best in St. Louis — survive.

This city does not hand out literary careers like party favors. It does not anoint. It endures. And the poets in this collection have endured right alongside it. They have read to packed houses, to six people, and to one distracted guy nursing a beer in the corner. They have read through heartbreak, day jobs, night shifts, bad reviews, good reviews, and the long silences in between.

I booked them because they were good. I kept booking them because I've never stopped believing in them.

What you hold in your hands is not a "scene" in the trend-piece sense of the word. It is something better. It is a small sample of a body of work forged in open mics, back rooms, bookstores, and bars — with too much booze, coffee, and/or anxiety running through us. It is argument and confession. It is humor sharpened into a blade and tenderness smuggled in under a joke.

If there is a common thread here, it is persistence. Not the glamorous kind. The kind that shows up anyway.

These poets have given more to their craft than can ever be quantified. I hope they know how grateful I have always been for every syllable they gave. This anthology is proof that the performance was never the point. It was the work. Always the work.

-Daniel W. Wright

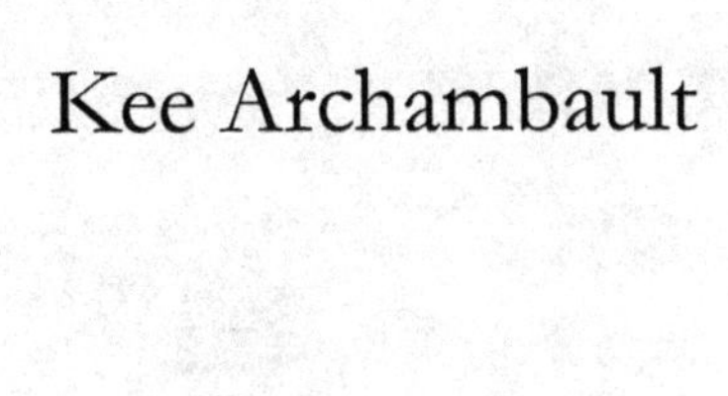

Kee Archambault

Kee Archambault (pronounced 'key ahr-shahm-BOH') is originally from remote northern California but has lived in St. Louis for approaching 20 years as of the publication of this book. Her writing includes themes such as consciousness, romantic love, and identity, and is informed by a childhood of significant social isolation, as well as her studies in the areas of biology, ecology, and evolution. She lives in the Tower Grove South neighborhood with her house rabbit, Rosie.

Personality

consider now
the dendritic core,
its branches dying off
and back,
to reach again
as it absorbs
and subsumes;
tendrils
evermore alight
upon an instance,
seeking, seeking
at the meeting
of intersected matrices,
particles
infinitely fine
and aligning,
just so;
the core recalls
its passenger,
ferrying hither
and thither
within space;
borne as it is reborn,
its multifaceted face
sheds its likeness
in momentous struggle
through time;

blooming layers unfurl
to fall away,
revealing what lies
beneath the overwhelming tide
of what's next.

The Curse

bereft of drawstrings,
I painted
a sticky,
scarlet scene.
a nurse made clear
my fated need,
causing my heart to bleed
for fifteen years;
locked into that
impossible quest,
I guess
that I'll sooner extinguish
the sun,
because I don't believe
in true love.

Crybaby

from the vector of my head
a scattershot of taught threads
strikes outward;
each terminus
an anachronistic tack,
pinning fine red lines
to a distorted reckoning map
of past lessons;
I superimpose
these ghostly gleanings
to cope with fleeting meetings
of ego and id,
because what my keepers couldn't do
was keep me safe
and clothed
and fed, and naturally,
this strategy fails,
and so I cry
much like a child,
but my bitter cries are quelled,
my manner mandatorily mild,
because never would I dare offend,
and I apologize and plead,
and I'll be sorry till I'm dead
if I can ask for what I need:
just please, don't yell at me
anymore.

Visions

up against
a spiking aura
made opaque by a haze
of proud ignorance,
I had been fascinated
by the potentiality
of shared experiences;
of roving boundless
to witness the strange
something
in which we find ourselves
immersed,
brutally elegant
and bursting cacophonous
to decay into obscurity,
just like us.
after all,
consciousness
means 'knowledge with',
and you know
how much I love
to share my nonsense.

Dilated

resignation and acceptance
giving way to the impossible present:
the precious tragedy
of time's conclusion
inexorable
when never again would we enfold
in scarred arms
or drink from pools of shining blackness
that were our eyes
dazzled by oxytocin and happenstance.

Headlong

running in all directions,
the pseudopodal sprawl
of my tenuous connections
seeking something radical:
your moonbow radiation
like a halo--
inspiration
arriving unannounced;
my magnesium fascination,
flaring at a gravitation
so precarious within its bounds;
our interface,
dynamic,
points of contact realigning,
redefining our terms
with reckless ingenuity.

Little

inauspiciously timed,
I find myself assailed
by the wailing of woes
long passed behind me;
ashamed of inarticulation,
and still preoccupied
with the implication
of all goodbyes,
I turn to see
that you have fled
from me
and all my little fears.

Lucky Break

the strain
of sustained affection
relents
and spreading in all directions,
I become amorphous and absurd;
I become unbothered and charismatic,
prismatic and preoccupied,
existential and concerned
with ladders
and spirals;
with enmeshments
and iterations;
with kaleidoscopic questions
of being,
and drunken intrigues
that belie my hold-out hopes
for ultimate dignity...
how fortunate to be
diverted by you
again.

Time As Lover

the scene I perceive
slides sideways,
misaligning
in ways without words,
and so I approximate:
to flicker,
shiver,
shift,
and blur,
axes inverting as,
like Future and Past,
we collide and caress,
obliged to our passing,
but ever learning
to express the present
as we yearn
for déjà vu.

Weirdos

I've felt it
time and time again,
each body a stand-in
to dispel my loneliness,
each failing
to impress upon me
an inclination
toward my frequency.
and so I wander,
collecting connections,
eschewing advice
to achieve saturation,
but it doesn't suffice.
what does it mean
to be deeply seen?
a recognition amidst
a swirling pool
of souls,
as vast
as it is oblivious
to its strangest currents;
a joining
of multiplicitous filaments,
connecting
to gleefully relay
so much
dubious wisdom.

T. James Chapman

T. James Chapman is a poet based on the southside of St. Louis, writing about the underbelly and underground of the Midwest, the places most would call "flyover country" in all it's surrealistic and grimy glory.

Rush Limbaugh is Buried in Bellfontaine

i hear there's cameras on rush limbaugh's grave
cause people were pissing on it
vandalizing it.
but i bought a ski mask
from walmart and a spade shovel and i reckon
he'd look real nice hung upside down
and paraded around just north of delmar.

Illuminated IKEA Due West of the Indoor Put-Put Place Before Sunrise Brings a Certain Magic to the Skyline While Wiping Sleep From the Bottom Corners of Your Eye & Praying the Next Drink of Monster Don't Taste Like the Bottom of the Can

you know, the air used to smell
of cinnamon rolls
til they took the flavored air away
insisting whimsy is found in the fall collection
there is still smiles to be found
in a platos closet
or saddled to the trough
at golden corral
passing moments to fuel an all-dayer
at the outlet malls
or fuel a half-dayer (if you're lucky)
at the pentacostal church in the stip mall
kind of a
kind of a meal saturday to get you fed

-spiritually speaking-
on a sunday

that sustains (if you're lucky)

for a whole week of traffic jams and time clocks

Death Poem I: Longing

a body withers
a spirit up & runs off
i coulda swore i caught
a bouquet at a wedding as a little one
now i snatch an orchid
off a coffin lid just before
that first shovel-full meets my head-hair
the dirt just misses again

pants-pockets brimming
with black flowers
i'm jealous of every mounded-over grave
a yet to rust spade shovel
leaned over top - leaves surrounding -
they would be crunchy if not
for the sweat of the gravedigger
the tears & blood of the mourners
are just a performance leaving
leaves bone dry

i dream of feral horses
causing pile-ups as they cross
two-lane highways unscathed
i crush a skunk
with my right-front tire
on the way to work

Interracial Lesbian Tweaker Couple in a Scrap Truck (I Can Say Tweaker Because I used to Manufacture and Smoke Meth (I've Also Sold Scrap for Rent Money))

the resale shop next door to my apartment complex
with the boarded up glass door
when it first opened
the man who ran it told me he closes at sunset
he closes at sunset because these young bucks

like to walk around in ski masks
and he don't wanna have to scrap with em like that
he wants this place to be community oriented
he gave me a t-shirt

the resale shop next to my apartment complex
is refuge for these two women of indiscriminate age
is it the hard livin or just genuine years?
either way they laugh all the way
to the boarded up glass door
a 4-wheel drive dodge left in the dust of south grand
a stretch of street that don't care if your suspension
is squatted in the back
suspension squatted for the scrap in the back
bowed down to a hard life and love found
at a kitchen table where tattoos
are freely given and there's a handle of ten high
on the counter for anyone brave enough to drink it

poor dodge left in the dust
step rail rusted clean off
so the most beautiful couple ive ever seen
jumps in after a good while of bargain hunting
at the resale shop

Do You Want to be Crushed Under an Amalgamation of Press Board and Laminate? Then You Best Not Climb Them Shelves!

middle class empathy smells like a rubber fishing
    worm
no spine or hands to wrestle that trophy fish called
    equity to shore
bloodstains on a river bank don't show from the
    highway
but blood is still spilt
blood's still spilt

What if Hamas Kidnapped Tarantino's Wife, Cut Off Her Feet and Mailed Them to Him?

my boy joe once told me
st. louis antifascism isn't sexy

like it is in portland
we face down pigs on state-streets
with no street lights

left hand stretched behind
an old recliner
clutching a 12ga. pump
one in the hole
ready
eager to talk to the plainclothes fed
at the front door

boosie yells out every car window:
without that badge you a bitch & a half
to communists with ski masks and long guns
to everyone else who got one in their waistband
to the crip facing ACA charges but is still in the mix

no one saw megan green at the repass
the one where the mom of the deceased
asked folks to stand ready with ARs
just in case the cops felt froggy again

the good reverend darryl gray
beat his wife nearly to death &
moved down here to get paid to tame us

he will die. rebellion will not.

opposing parties meet for brunch
in the new ballroom
at the white house:
mamdami our savior!
cori bush our savior!
but nikki giovani – god rest her soul –
nikki giovani said:
the barrel of a gun is the best voting machine

but we don't read her words
just share posts in her memory
so we soil that memory
we piss on the grave of revolutionary women
a white liberal piss that adds no ammonia
no vigor
a piss that waters us down just enough
so when the white hot bleach of reaction rains down
there is no mustard gas
only words
only t-shirts

Death Poem III: Acceptance

it could be any two folks on this road right now
but i'm glad it's us.
i'm glad the right-front tire is bald
and i'm glad that these vultures fly in circles.
an air show just for us.

**I Didn't Want to Get Into a Shootout in the
Ozarks, They had Murder on Their Mind
and They Were All Doing it for God**

potato soup's bubbling on a
old electric stove.
you can feel the heat off the big front coil

starch in the air smells like the holy ghost
there's three books on a shelf:

the bible
a cookbook
and some fella's diary

a paper towel tube -bare as adam in genesis -
hangs on a dowel mounted
crooked to panel'd walls

sweat drip drops onto my bolo tie
(fake turquoise from some second hand store)
shoulda wore an undershirt.
this collar'd one is see-thru now

i grew up poor and skeptical
wonder how ida turned out if i hadn't
found that punk rock tape in my cousin's chest-of-
    drawers
it had the same fake walnut veneer

as this dining room table.
same plastic ashtray centerpiece too
i want to interogate the system
i want to blame don imus
but maybe some folks are just assholes

Return to Sender/Address Unknown/No Such Person/No Such Zone

i'm a postage stamp on a queen size bed
a peninsula jutting
into empty bottles
& taco bell bags
this envelope ain't going nowhere
won't even make it to the post office

i write an address i write it again
i don't know the numbers or road
i write the address in night sweat
on sheets that need washing
the DTs long left me, but still
the shakes persist

the sheets pool with sweat & makes me cold
thee sweat absorbs by morning
& a sink bath sends me off to work

**I Couldn't Find An Elvis Song to Quote,
So Here:**

after work i build a chest of drawers
while you sweat at a lousy job
i stare at the threads pulling from my work flannel
& imagine the clothes you'd create
from what i destroyed

pine boards make a fine chest
make a fine coffin too
i'm glad these boards will hold your sweaters
& thankful there's room for my threadbare flannel

Jesse Eikmann

Jesse Eikmann is a trans man poet and editor native to St. Louis but currently residing in Wisconsin. He got an MFA in poetry from University of Missouri-St. Louis in 2019, was abducted thereafter by the St. Louis indie scene, and now spends his time editing and beta reading his friends' goofy indie manuscripts and hustling on the local open mic circuit. Jesse is the author of *First, a Crisis* (Back of the Class, 2024) and *The Kiss of Complicity* (Bad Jacket Press, 2019).

Powerball

It's day three of this. I can barely stand to look at them. Masses practically to the back wall of Kwik Trip. They come to the counter with numbered balls ricocheting in their bingo cage brains. 1.6 billion: a big number mumbled by small people with even smaller margins for failure. Mortgage under water. Trading meals for orange paper. Separate tickets. Power play. I'm playing with my health care. Same but different. I'm gambling I can put off my surgery two more months. If I'm lucky it's 10 grand. If not the cost is the least of my problems. They flood the store all night. A cluster of guys sifting singles from dry-wall dusted overalls. Flock of dishwater blondes in 12 shades of the same hoodies and yoga pants. Friday afternoon regular with a 30-pack of Hamm's and an oxygen tank in his cart. Different but the same. They don't want the receipt. They joke that *as long as I get the winner I don't need it.* They'll buy everyone in town a house. They'll tip me 10 grand if they don't forget me. They'd forget everyone immediately. They'd have 1.6 billion reasons not to remember. My boss says she's buying herself an island. Fun and games until your living room's under water. I've been under water all year. 1.6 billion won't buy me buoyancy but maybe it'll help the other small people float. Caged brains. They gamble with their rent. They gambled with my rights. They play with power at the ballot box because it's the next best thing if you don't have 1.6 billion. The machine wheezes out more orange paper. I snatch the slip and finally snap: *Nobody deserves a goddamn billion dollars!*

The Opposite of Tits

A seam on my oldest bra has officially blown,
its opening contorted in an *oh* of protest. And I say,
girl, same. I wish she could see
there's a fixed date
on my calendar where she will be
blissfully pink-slipped from her Sissy-phean position.
Many before her have failed.
How could they not? Nobody could crush
these dumb puppies enough to keep men
from noticing with such gusto on the subway
or get them apoplectic in the men's room.
So I'll give her a deal:
she keeps it together for four months
and I'll plan her one hell of a retirement party.
She'll be the antithesis
of everything her CEOs slouched for,
the opposite of tits. Wanna slingshot
these motherfuckers at my mom
when she clings religiously to this obscene
lie that my genes bequeathed me? Go for it.
Wanna lasso a glass of milk
out of a kid's hand mid-sip
so I can go to Planned Parenthood
and pour a libation
to the infertility goddess? Done.
I'll even promise that when I burn her,
when she can finally stop pushing back and

let the fire overwhelm her,
I won't recoil when the sour sweat
smell gets released from her band
like zombies from the crypt. It's not her fault,
and with all these years of quiet quitting she's done,
it's the least I could do.

Trans At Their Expense

Being trans isn't the Riddle of the Sphinx to block
cis admission to anything, or a Molotov cocktail
thrown to set normal interactions ablaze. But my
hot take? Even if it was scandal by design, I'd love
it. Soaking up other people's panic when I turns
around on a sales floor, telling them where our milk
is as if I didn't hear "ma—I mean, oh god, sorry sir."
Giggling when a hotel guest compliments my beard,
then saying "Thanks, I cheated!" as the elevator doors
close around his confusion. Staring down a stranger's
car window, hearing the tired siren song "you got a
man?" and then the hysterical lurch of his tires when
I snarl, "I *am* a man." It's a perfect monkey wrench,
a gender-bender-conversation-ender. I wish I tried it
years ago, before I even guessed it was the truth. So
many shameful silences I could have blown open, so
many thoughtlessly tossed barbs I could have hurled
right back. In another life I wouldn't have dreamed of
quarantining my short dresses after toothless losers
screamed across the street, "How much you selling
that ass for?" I'd know to answer, "Enough to send my
boobs on vacation to Texas but not enough to bring
them back. How's that?"

If my gender's a bomb
I won't defuse or hide it
to soothe anyone.

A Ghost, to Another of Their Kind

I see you're on your semi-yearly haunt
of my inactive OKCupid page.
Your wife dispensed one senseless slug of rage
too many, and you left. But what you want—
no-strings-attached big tits, hips, floral skirt
abandoned in the fabric of your bed—
these relics of the feminine are dead
or soon to die. I guess that must have hurt
your boner, since you never did respond,
retreating to your unresponsive mist
to grieve the toy that won't simply exist
when you're bored. How ironic you were conned
by phantom presences from my old host,
a ghost tricked into lusting for a ghost.

Portrait of Us with No Northern Lights

"Remember, we're looking for motion," she says, "not just a change in the light." As if a pulse of periwinkle or neon green is going to arrest me, to hold my attention enough to say *this is why I'm here*. I'm not looking for aurora borealis, and clearly it's not looking for us. She's draped over the driver's side of her Toyota, sifting the gray light in the west, filtering out stars and the crimson twitches of air traffic. I'm hiding under the east side of the sky, the only part that betrays the late hour. My palm lights up every few seconds like a firefly: someone missing me from 800 miles away. In between checking that, my eyes are hailing every pair of headlights traveling anywhere else. Someplace where sunset's ass-end isn't still lagging at 10:30. Or somewhere so far south that I won't be dragged from bed multiple times in one week to hunt half-heartedly for a few stripes of sky highlighter. She says we'll call it soon, but for ten minutes we tarry there, separated by a car body and emptiness, each pursuing unrelated motion and light.

The Peony, and Everything that Blooms

is as vulnerable as it is beautiful.
The peonies overflourished
in the summer rain, and rain
humbled them for it. The bush
wound up storm-seamed,
magenta and blush
blooms so slumped
to the ground the bees forgot
their wings and crawled
to the carpels.
I wondered how much
time I had left, how long
to be heavy
with this improbable
happiness, before my back
goes crooked with a new crisis
and someone flies in, harvests
what little is left to grind it
to dust in hundreds
of greedy hands. How long
until I end up like these
post-mortem petals,
layers of blotted red
tongues brittle from
exposure
at the edge. They shriveled,
and so will summer, spread now

like an empress across the whole day
but destined to curl concave
like a kidney and fall
off its throne.
And I will disappear with it,
or it with me, and no one
will know if my black and
severed tongue is the mirror
or the four-thirty darkness around me
is the mirror, or whether it was better
to have stayed upright
in a hard green ball and never
revealed anything at all.

My Love Was Free Because
Someone Else Paid for It

At 19, I turned from the last straggles of smoke from my first affair and became an arsonist. I carried a torch to every spoken-for man I could get, let him touch it, and watched his world catch fire. That whole year, I thought nothing of it. I felt no sadness when the thirty-something café owner in my therapist's building pulled out in a parking garage, and I asked him about the car seat nestled next to a McDonald's bag in the back. He was dribbling into a sock. His answer somehow bound *eighteen-month-old, fiancée,* and *it's not serious* into one sentence. No hesitation when I met a man at a conference and let him burn from Wichita at an image of my thigh after a shower, my wrapped bath towel suggesting the rest, so much he messaged *Got it. And you're evil.* I didn't even blink when I stood in the same bathroom, working on my smirk in the mirror as I said *I don't care, I don't have anyone to answer to anymore, just dump him if you're that mad* to a strange woman on the phone.

I can't tell you what finally snuffed me out. It wasn't getting older, as Mr. It's Not Serious can show you. I can picture his midlife, him trying to spark the wet ashes of his marriage and then unseriously depositing his wedding ring in his pocket, dipping into a teenager's jeans. I can't even say for sure when the bubble of my young hot rage gave way to simmering wisdom. But my when and why are smokescreens that don't matter and haven't mattered in years; what does matter is the women. The unaware mother invoked as casually as the takeout trash was tossed. The one confronting me from Kansas. I bet she saw through me, the nihilism I bummed off some movie, the *evil* brand whose sting I wouldn't feel until later. These days that's the only thing in me that burns, the psoriatic scorch of remorse when I recall how easy it all was, how you can hussy so hard you can cover your own combustion for a while. And how criminal it was that I could start those fires and my lungs never blackened with the aftermath.

Slow Burns

I grab my latest with two fingers and hold it
up to the light. Prismatic diagonals
running through the perfect burnish
as I tilt the bottom.
Number four-hundred-whatever. I lost track last summer
after I built the CD cabinet and thought
960 should take me a while.
I tell on myself
every time I kneel
like a monk
and slide another into the stacks.
Or, not a monk. They wouldn't insist on
stuffing all their silences with the sounds
of CD burning. But yes, I'm obsessed,
the dentist-drill whine at first,
the settled purr
on the last tracks,
the progress bar slogging
to the right. 50 blanks on my shelf,
and they'd be gone tomorrow if not
for a strict ritual, one a week
so it never has to end.

But they aren't flings to flirt with once
and leave. My stereo
turns them into old romances,
rekindled as many times as they'll take me.

There are stress fractures on my Jeff Buckley
from icy nights
when I crawl into bed and listen
to the same ten serenades
I'll never get tired of.
I tense up
in sympathy as "Mojo Pin" begins
—a man could have his body lacerated
every day for a hundred years
and still never pour
that much feeling in those *oohs*.

And maybe I take too much from these trysts,
maybe I'll pay for it on later playback,
but I always turn ten into eleven
because I can't resist
circling back to "Eternal Life."
It isn't the intended end,
but it's *my* end, and Jeff Buckley obliges
with the flickering
of the bass and the word   *angel*
held out at the outro.
It curls up the octaves
like a wisp of smoke,
the song floats into sweet silence,
and when I snip the disc from its spindle,
I need it to know
it's not the last goodbye.

Jill Firns

Jill Firns is a queer poet and aspiring novelist in St. Louis. As a youngster, she once had a re-imagination of "Roses are Red…" published in the *St. Louis Post Dispatch* and has been interested in writing ever since. She is a devoted attendee of Undercurrent, a weekly poetry workshop lead by internationally-recognized slam poet Desiree Dallagiacomo, and has had work published in *Preposition: The Undercurrent Anthology*. Through heavy imagery and storytelling masquerading as poetry, she explores relationships with the natural world, with others, and with the self.

How To Make a Peanut Butter and
Jelly Sandwich

The priest at my grade school used to say that the
Holy Trinity is like a peanut butter and jelly sandwich:

all parts exist individually and yet combine into
    something
more beautiful, more magnificent than we can fathom.

First, you take the bread. It doesn't matter what kind,
as long as it's soul-filling and pure,

and you arrange it neatly on a plate. Next,
spread peanut butter onto one slice of bread.

Be careful not to make a mess—
cleanliness is next to godliness, you know—

and sticky fingers are aligned with idle hands:
those who crave endlessly are seldom missed.

Thirdly, smear jam of your choice (Father Rauch
preferred grape, I think) onto the other slice.

The ratio must be perfect so as to ensure that no
drips happen when you bite into the sandwich, for

no holiness exists outside of The Big Three.
Lastly, gently lay the two slices together, folding

them together like you do your hands in prayer.
Like my grimy grade school fingers clapping together

to crush a small fly that flew too close to my face.
The sound carves through the church's quiet halls.

Other school children giggle, but I pay them no mind.
I instead daydream of the Seraphim.

How many sandwiches does one Seraphim need to
power all six wings? And do they prefer grape or
    strawberry

or blueberry or peach or rhubarb? Do they like the tart
taste of sinners' tears? Or do they yearn for the silken

souls of innocent children, kneeling on hard benches,
trying to pay attention through sleep-smeared eyes?

An Anaphora | Tower Grove Park at 7:07 p.m.

The park is pregnant, just short of bursting forth,
flush with a verdant renaissance led by snowdrops.

The catalpa trees blush with buds, the magnolias
shimmy their fuzzy pods in the blue hour's draft.

Fog will soon descend, wrapping wispy tongues
around trunks, lapping at branches full of secrets.

If you stand just perfectly still, you can almost hear
the rustle of the owl's neck feathers as its head twists.

You can almost hear the soft snap of underbush as
the coyote steps into the clearing, ears like feverish
    satellites.

You can almost hear the humming of the sheer veil
    between
day and dusk, a veil under which hides the evening's
    prey.

The earth quakes, just short of bursting at the seams,
expectant with the musty ripeness of ready soil.

The tennis courts are flush with players; the chain fence
shakes its links in the impact of a wayward ball.

Lights will flicker on, washing illumination over
trails, chasing birds into the trees where secrets
        are held.

And if you stand perfectly still, you can almost hear
the sigh of the city as it leaks creatures and citizens
        into the night.

green and wild things

When I feel lost, I return to my center,
to nature, just as I have done today.
I am basking on a boulder, flanked by running tendrils,
burbling and gurgling the secrets of upstream.
Rivulets of fragrant river gossip as they crawl over
my submerged toes; the rest of me spread across
this water-slicked rock worn silky with age.
Two hawks drift far above me on plumes of
air, floating in concurrent circles, overlapping
each other on an invisible axis.
Do they whisper to each other as
they pass in the sky?

The clouds knit themselves together in a
mesmerizing manner and I think of the day I left.
I ponder loss, and hope.
I have discovered it is easier to think about
them while amongst green and wild things.
I took both along with a prayer and a single suitcase.

A fly hovers just above my forehead before
darting away, vanishing between piles of
rustic rubble soaked in a summer storm's run-off.
I think about leaving, and healing.
It is comfortable, I have learned,
to slide into a stream of water and
let it wash away the brokenness.

I left it behind when I ran towards healing.
My reverie is broken by the sound of laughter:
a tinkling, joyous sound that harmonizes with
the riversong. A couple floats by, one half of the
sweet pair holding the other aloft in the water.
Belly-up, breasts thrust towards the soft mountains
of clouds above, I am light as a feather, stiff as a
board—she bobs gently. The honey is thick
    between them.
My heart reaches for the golden thread.
As I bask, I think about love.

There are a lot of things I am in love with right now,
but you are no longer one of them.

A Flash in the Room; Lightning

8.2.16

51

You have managed to sleep through
the last four out of four nighttime storms
that have ambled down my alleyway
The vibrato of your breath, face turned away from
     mine,
tells me that the thunder has not dragged you from
     slumber
by the ear as a mother pinches her tow-headed child
over a broken curfew.

The dog shifts beside my legs, yawns, twists,
presses against me with her two front paws,
against your waist with her two back paws.
She is splitting us into halves across the quilted
field of dreams that I am grasping at -

a swift, glassy memory of the Zoo
a walk in a grocery store, hand-in-hand
a bottle of bright white wine crashing to the floor
a hike effortlessly executed across quicksand, feet bare
a memory passed unknowingly from you to me
(she sits on the floor, applying makeup)

In a cocoon of 300 thread count
I am but a floating spirit, waiting always for you
to stir and smile, to set your Botticelli eyes upon

my face where I hover, slightly soul-separated,
anchored just so above the bed by the
crook of your pinky in mine.

white whales

My father crunches his long limbs into the passenger
    seat
and I wonder how much of his head touches the ceiling.
My own hair grazes the fabric of the 4Runner and
I glance at his hat, just a whisper away from the lining.

I am dropping him off at a mechanic shop to retrieve his
Lexus—money down the drain to save perhaps a dying car.
We make our usual small talk, and in the silence, I think
    about Captain Ahab.

Much like the sea, our connections to parents are ever-
    changing.
We chase in others the things that they cannot or will
    not offer.

I've learned this from the relationships I try not to view
    as "failed."
The ones with harpoons that dragged me into the
    depths.
The ones that yielded oil that burned and burned.
The ones that were beautiful, magnificent creatures
    destined to destroy.

We must be careful what we chase.

After all, a white whale is the thing that will drown you.

A Smattering of Nature Poems After Reading Mary Oliver's Collection Devotions

The cardinal begins his hardy cry
the moment I walk out the door,
The pattern of its voice sounding
like "hey pretty, pretty, pretty, pretty."
I bask in the sung compliments.
I feign tossing my hair over my shoulder.
Oh to be admired by that which Mother Nature
    already adores!

—— —— ——

The California wren carries its harvest to
the flower pot swinging on the back porch,
a cavity nester moving with haste.

The female has chosen this location,
at the behest of the male who
sang his song of confidence and approval.

The craftsmanship is exemplary
as the nest grows day by day.

Eventually, this bundle houses eggs—
three of which vanish and one of which stays.
I think on abandonment in the sly early morning
    shimmer.

Sometimes all I know is this:
you cannot take your troubles with you (when you're
    gone)

— — —

I ask my friend for one of her ceramic objects,
and she asks back "which kind?"

For there are bowls of beauty,
mugs of marvel, plates of posture.
Each crafted by loving hands,
imprinted with care and curiosity for
the shape they become while worked from wet clay.

I answer "mainly mugs :)" because there is
nothing more comforting than the steam of
tea tickling my face as my fingers wrap around
the pregnant base of a handmade cup's belly.

I do not ask for much - mostly simple pleasures.

— — —

The morning is thick with the simple quietude that
waterfront properties hold. A heron wings silently over
the speckled surface of the inlet, flapping three times
then gliding, and I imagine it is sliding its belly along
a sheer glass tabletop, using its feather fingers to push
itself swiftly along. After all, do the clouds not swoosh
along the invisible surface of our nearest atmosphere?

A sound breaks the stillness and I cannot see what makes it, but it is moving closer. All at once, they're in view, slicing the watertop with slick blades of silvery flesh. And with each exhalation comes a "booosh" - a whooshing sound from their blowholes. Four dolphins surfacing in intervals as they travel further in-land, dark bodies dispersing the water in the early morning shift of sun. I rush to the dock to view them. The sky bleeds pink to yellow to blue. I watch until they turn the corner, straining to hear their breath over the sound of my own.

The Seven Deadly Sorrows

I.
Eyes upward; palms lifted. The first sword enters the
right chamber, piercing plainly and cleanly. A holy
wound: one without blood to stain her heavy chest.
Strike down that which feeds the ego.

II.
Gaze lowers; fingers grasping. A second sword cruises
through cloth and flesh—another angle altogether.
The taste of avarice in her mouth: spittle trickles over
her lips. Savor the drip that drowns out the dreaming.

III.
Fists curl; jaw clenches. The third spike finds its mark,
pulsing forth a deeper crimson river of chastisement.
A fury bursts above her head: a crown fully aflame.
Curse out the passion and pain of celestial animation.

IV.
Head lolls; ears burn. A fourth blade cracks bone on
entrance, releasing a deep need for similarity. Gowns
of silk, of gold, of umbered riches: the narrative of
another. Relinquish the want for that which is not
your own.

V.
Legs open; breasts heave. The fifth penetration
begins, an earthquake of unsanctimonious origins
threatening to unfold from deep within. Ask Cupid
to relent: only the meek will inherit the earth's center.

VI.

Mouth opens; teeth gnash. A sixth sharp finds its
mark, drawing out a cry for more, more, more:
another, another, another! Bury your shame in the
depths, hidden beneath the folds of self-negligence.

VII.

Eyes lower; hands soften. The seventh dagger
determines the final space: squirming slowly in
determination to escape, albeit unceremoniously.
Languishing: sighing in the dimming light.

Lay down your soft body, transfixed.

Twelve Oysters

sit atop sparkling shaved ice,
a picture-perfect promenade of
flesh ripe with the essence of desire.

We eat them in the lingering sun,
your hair shimmering on your shoulders
as your lashes lower to watch
the oysters slide from shell to tongue.

In my experience, aphrodisiacs have never
been necessary for flirtation; they are not required
for our mouths to find each other in the dark.

Heat vs. Humidity | August 21, 2020

Dryness is something that I take for granted. The
    beads
of sweat on my skin feel different in Southwestern
    heat and I would
rather they evaporate on their own than fall to the
    earth.

Feeling dwarfed by nature is not something I take
    lightly.

People ask me:
"Are you more of an ocean person or a mountain
    person?"
How can it be an either - or when I stand in the
sediment silt of ancient oceans whose underwater
    cliffs
became the nesting bluffs of Triassic, winged
    creatures
whose Latin name means "heavenly wind?"

Thriving in a desert is much like shedding your
    skin —
you must become more reptilian than ever, following
    instinct
yet staving off the urges to slither wildly across the
    sand,
barely touching the ground, winding and writhing
    under fallen trees.

There is nothing to prove if there is no one to prove
    it to.
Your skin only belongs to you. Gather it each season,
    tuck it
into a glass jar and display it on your mantelpiece.

In fact, the shedding rather scares me the most.

It's the promise of becoming your full self —
the one that feels too big to fit into the glass jar.
You bubble over, the cork that kept you inside
bursting from the top. It bounces from wall to window
and ricochets off the ceiling fan. The skin you shed in
    order
to become —

Well, now that's your sustenance.
You must consume yourself to become.
You are an ouroboros.
You are a serpent with no end.

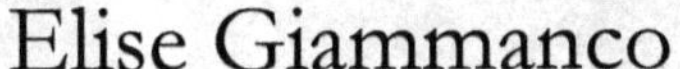
Elise Giammanco

Elise Giammanco is a poet originally from the St. Louis area who now resides in Mount Shasta, CA. Her work has appeared *Bad Jacket Magazine*.

A Dictionary of Beasts

My intuition is bright like these
Floodlights on the front porch
Hugging every curve of my body
We must look out for bears and men
Mostly men
Dried lavender and lenticulars
Sacramento headwaters
Mother mountain is big
She has room for everyone
She begs us to be kind
I see dying dreams
New ones burgeoning
Bearing witness to
What is becoming

Saturate

Father goes to the well in the morning
Mother goes to the well at night
Sister goes to the well at sunset
Brother goes to the well at sunrise
I got to the well and weep at the sight
All the taking without a drop of relief
I'll water the well and take none for me

Lady Weed

Don't "Lady" me!
Lady, let's just wait and see.
Miss "I don't know if I can wait another week"
Hindrance
Chokehold
Dumb
The lines I wish I would've written down when I was
    in the bathtub

Slowest Love in the World

Like my 1960s drip coffee maker
Even slower and hotter
Albuquerque traffic at 7am
Sunshine leaking over the Sandias
Blinding, building, maddening
A blown tire in the middle of the desert
Never know if you're gonna get a tow
I have never seen love this up close
It hasn't been this easy before like Bob said
I think about you all of the time
And then I can't help it to think of you
Once more
I'm splitting the seconds
Waiting until you pay attention
You always eventually do
I see the signs, I am wide enough
Now what about the miracle

Like shooting a butterfly

There you go again
Looking for meaning
This violence is nonsense, no logic
It doesn't matter if you drive through
Truth and Consequences, New Mexico
At midnight, at sunrise or
On a Wednesday afternoon
You can sit by the Rio Grande
Way down in Hatch
After buying a strand of hot chilis
Dangling, crisp and glimmering
Scarlet, lime green, colors of love
Stale and jealous, throw up sick
(I have $1, Please take it!)
Time is your best friend
That keeps making the same mistakes
What he did to you
Nothing but a power trip
Fumbling the sun
Freezing around warmth
Today, I am in the mountains
There is no one here shooting at me
Only the stars above the snow-capped ridges

Maxim(s)

I ought to wake up early in order to
Flounder in finishing my work (always)
In order to come home before sunset
In order to kiss your lips more
I want to test for perfect duties
And imperfect ones, too
Some changes I can't make
On my own, although

I ought to sell my own horses
In order to afford my own dowry
In order to give away my own
Dappled disasters called dreams
The backs of my divorced hands
Along with the unfamiliar parts
Seashells of my life's meaning
Washed up on your shoreline

I ought to write about us more
In order to prehistorically stumble
Into some higher moral standard
Guided by fault-line feeling
Some other big bang theory yet
Informed by only the soundest
Of actions and tactile philosophy

I ought to work out the mathematics
In order to perform at the highest level
To push motion in a certain direction
To grow tomatoes in a garden
In order to miss the phone calls that
I will undoubtedly miss while eating them barefoot with
    you in the backyard
Sweet, savory juices running down our smiling mouths

Something I think I have to name:
Love / Unbeknownst to me until now

Silicosis

Don't tell me you didn't see no dust!
The closest thing to unforgivable is slavery
You made me dirty
Treated me like a machine
Give me your tired, give me your poor
I'll put you in a grave
And you'll be ignored
For generations and generations
While yearning to be free
As the rich remain the comparative few
All the while becoming disjointed as a country
And dishonored by the bloodshed
Workers have rights
And life is all about sex and money
While being gradually regimented into nothing
That is the history of America
Conscious of its ignorance
It's distorted visions of reality
In no way true or passionate or honest
You cannot scrub away the blood
Off of that West Virginian mountain
You cannot unbury the dead
In the Louisiana swamplands
You cannot put a nice bow around death
And then say everything is better now

Collecting Civilians

"A pair of classic Levi 501s," he said
"A polo or two
Oh! A pair of classic boat shoes
Brown Sperrys, you know the ones
And I've been thinking about it
For quite a while now
If you have the time
Could you find me a watch?
It's been 17 years since I've gotten to wear one,
    ya know?"

Natural Selection

Once the blackberries are picked
"One must always choose,"
I whisper softly to myself
Must I edit out the most
Delectable bits of pith?
Which berry in the bunch
Do I dare devour first?
Swiftly, slowly, in-between
The place and time
They don't matter as much
Was it happenstance
Or was it always you?

Zaire Imani

Zaire Imani has been a poet in St. Louis for over 25 years. Her work has been lauded by Washington University, and she has performed all across the country. She has opened for The Roots, Gil Scott-Heron, and Digable Planets. Zaire has appeared at the National Poetry Slam seven times, placing sixth in the nation.

honesty

my third eye vibrates wildly
but sometimes I stare vacantly
because my peace has been taken from me
and now I need reassurity
and search for security
laving you feeling lost
and you won't come and find me
but you'll never lose me
because what god has joined together
no man can separate
and hate will not devour me.

I search desperately for you beneath your
armour of defense and see you behind your
curtain of resistance.
Your silhouette to me is beautiful
it incites my desire to see the true you
the fearless you.

Searching for you I take to the streets
i'm kicking broken bottles beneath my feet
vibrations being blocked by asphalt and concrete
in this here jungle seems everyone's asleep
under spells of devil's dreams
and I hear the screams of souls
precariously perched at purgatory's pinnacle.

Frustration and aggression
and steady stressin's
got you straddling fences
of liberation and self-oppression
straddling spiked fences squashing sacs
and cutting cords that link to source
vibrant, pulsating cord that carries life-force
red and heavy like four scarlet letters around my neck
replacing five elekes from past life.

Around my neck I wear your love locket
like an albatross
and on my shoulder I bear your cross
next to my own
on my throne I now feel alone and
my queendom is bound to fall
I am the bearer of all your bad decisions
and the bearer of your sweetly spilled seeds
still complacently meet what you drag in
from the street.
At your feet I weep
washing salty toes with my tears and locks
I am mary magdalene
released seven demons and a lifetime of fear
to be whole for you
i'm mary, black madonna
you fill your lungs with my prahna
you suck my air and I sacrifice my breath for you
give my breathed to be sucked and swirled
into your universe

your microcosmic bottomless pit
that longs to be filled with life
with light.

You suck my life-force
my energy
sometimes leaving me empty
it's like i'm drowning and you
drowning sorrows in bacardi bottles
you pour libations to your demons and they're
screaming for more
knock-knock-knocking on hades' door
and you whore your jaded love
for prone pussy non-resistance
keeping commitment at a distance.

Clean up my mess and suck in my stress
and maybe i'll go home a changed man
spilling seeds of sour sorrow
and long lost morals
between white thighs, but
I am the harvester of your lies
I am you wife
I am your christ
I gave you my breath
I gave you my life
but tell me honestly
what did you give me?

I've Had You

I've had you on my mind
99.9 percent of the time
for the last five years
I've had your taste in my tears
and my hopes and fears revolve around you
if you are the sun then I am the moon
reflecting your light giving rise to the tides
of our sacred Waters
I am the earth
giving birth to your daughters
my fertile dirt gives life consistently
to even the most wantonly spilled the seeds
like pure light I've had you
melt between my arms
filling me with the glows of your charms
illuminating me from the inside out
so much that I forget all about
the blinding darkness the keeps me traveling
down the same wrong road
I've had you tell me you love me
in moments of ecstasy
through Tantric telepathy
I've had you so deeply inside me that for a moment
I became you fucking me
and finally I knew how it felt to love
myself
I've had you in my dreams when I'm sleeping
recurrent themes that you're creeping

and I like to think even though I have a degree in
    prophecy
these dreams don't apply to me
a reflection of my insecurity
perhaps a sadistic fantasy
and I've had you telling
me that really nothing's happening
and mine's only ass your waxin'
but-
every week you knock my world off its axis
and I wish I could put the earth into stasis
stop it from spinning on Monday nights
holding it tightly in my grip
until Wednesday's dawn
so that Tuesdays would never come
no Mars day to fuel the rage
that I repress in your presence
I confess and do penance
for your transgressions
just so there'll be some sort of reconciliation
seems my aggression is a futile frustration
because I've never really had you
all to myself
no,
I'm like a book that you put on the shelf
when the story gets boring
or the theme too complex
then it's onto the next book
the one with the larger print
and less attractive cover
but is always a good lover-

er- I mean read
when all you really need
is mind-numbing fluff and fiction
but back to reality
I've had you
hand me rationalizations and technicalities
that don't even matter to me
because my love stretches far beyond the boundaries
of logic and reason
my wounded soul is just a petty consequence
for your treason
my tears a mere inconvenience
because today it seems treachery is in season
and lechery is just par for the course
of course I've had you
but only in parts mine is just another bleeding heart
pierced by the stake you refer to as your dick
it seems I've fallen for the trick
and I knew the game was unfair
when I decided to play
but for some reason I did anyway
and now it's checkmate for me because in reality
I can't check my mate
and player I'm hating your game
you see, I thought the object was to protect the queen
but apparently we weren't on the same team
I was black you were white
the two of us like day and night
neither existing without the other
my lover
but your tactics I can't bear them

and your harem…
I know they're just pawns in your game
but it still burns just the same
so tell me how do I settle for parts of a fragmented
    whole
must I sell my soul
for these token pieces of affection
and the inconsistent attention
that a oundaryless whore
would settle for?
There's so much more that I'm worthy of
and now it seems
there's not enough love in the galaxy
to fill this void in my physicality
the shards of your deception
and mistrajectories of your affection
have wounded my soul and yet
somehow I remain whole
I've had you so much that I've had it with you
because to you one plus one was always two
instead of one unit unified
like 1×1
I multiplied
and now have you inside my cells forever
perhaps never to own my singularity
because now our plurality has become my
quantum reality
so ultimately
I will always have you
even if I never really had you.

Light, sound, energy-

Bodies collide rhythmically
outwardly explosive
inward implosions
two microcosmic worlds
joining to create
one
vast universe of expansion
cells multiply and divide
inside
the valley
of my ripeness
cradle of darkness
illuminated
by the light of
life
resting place
and growing space
for resurrected souls
within me
the mystery
of
LIFE
unfolds.

Heather Kays

Heather Kays is a St. Louis–based poet and author. Her memoir Pieces of Us examines her mother's struggles with alcoholism and addiction, and her young adult novel *Lila's Letters* explores healing through unsent letters. Her debut poetry collection, *Myths in the Feed*, sold out six times in three months, making her Crying Heart Press's best-selling author. She was nominated twice for the Pushcart Prize in 2025. Heather runs The Alchemists, an online writing group and creative community, and is drawn to stories that explore survival, identity, and the complexity of being human. Her work has appeared in *ONE ART*, *Cosmic Daffodil Journal*, *Chiron Review*, *The Literary Underground*, *The Rye Whiskey Review*, *SHINE Poetry Series*, and *McSweeney's Internet Tendency*.

What I've Learned in St. Louis

I have learned that small-town gossip doesn't need a
    small town.
It thrives just fine in the shadow of skyscrapers,
trickling down brick alleys,
whispered over coffee cups that hold more bitterness
    than caffeine.
I have learned that cliques wear adult clothes here,
their laughter sharp and their criticism sharper.
For some people, tearing others down is their only
    form of construction.
I have learned that I am always just a little out of place,
like a song in the wrong key,
a little too loud,
too soft,
too much,
not enough.
I fill the space between "what we were expecting"
and "this is good because it is real."
I have learned that fair-weather friends wear high-
    thread-count disguises.
They hug you warmly, kiss your cheek,
and step aside when the storm clouds gather.
I have learned that art isn't a hobby here—
it's sustenance.
There are people who eat, sleep, and breathe it,
who bleed paint,
speak in lyrics,

and leave trails of poetry like breadcrumbs behind
    them.
They are the reason this city hums,
even when it seems to be falling asleep.
I have learned that St. Louis has no concept of pizza.
They'll hand you some kind of cracker with cheese
    on it
and call it a day.
But their gooey butter cake might make you believe
    in miracles.
I have learned that some of the best music you'll
    ever hear
won't be on a stage with perfect lighting.
It'll be in the back of a dive bar
whose name you forgot as soon as you left,
with a band you'll never find on Spotify,
but who left a mark on your soul anyway.
I have learned that strangers can become family
faster than some families deserve to.
And that people you thought would be around
    forever
can disappear so completely
you'll wonder if you imagined them.
I have learned that warnings about someone
can sometimes be the most dangerous thing of all.
The people who want to isolate you
often fear the light you might find
if you see the world for yourself.
I have learned that most of the hot men in St. Louis
    aren't worth the effort.

Their mere existence is their gift to the world—or so
    they think.
They'll offer you lukewarm lines,
just enough to make sure you still want them.
It's dumb. Don't feed into it.
I've learned I don't want to be a fluffer for a fragile
    male ego.
I've learned that not just any kind of dick will do—
    it has to be the right kind.
I have learned that liberation is not the same as
    loneliness,
but they often hold hands for a while.
I have learned that loving yourself
is sometimes the loudest act of rebellion.
I have learned that cities can be both cages and
    cathedrals.
That sometimes you pray to leave,
and sometimes you kneel to stay.
I have learned that this city can smell like beer and
    regret,
or rain on old bricks,
or hope.
That no two streets tell the same story,
but every one of them has something to say.
I have learned that survival is an art form here,
and I am becoming a master of it.

This City Sings Me Home

I came here restless, heart bruised and homesick for
something I couldn't name— a place, a purpose, a
pulse. And then I found you: a poetry scene drunk on
passion, fierce with fire, where words spark like flint
on steel.

You, bold as a revolution— shouting truth into the
dark until it echoes back belief. You, delicate as lace
yet unyielding— spinning tenderness into unbreakable
threads. You, fierce like a summer storm— lightning
in your veins, thunder in your voice. You, sweet as
honey but sharp-edged— a blade hidden beneath a
smile.

Together, we build something holy— a cathedral of
verse, a sanctuary of sound. Each stanza a shared
heartbeat, each line a lifeline thrown in trust. We've
made art from ashes, love from language, and family
from fire.

I never expected to belong like this— held in the arms
of strangers who became soulmates, raised up by the
brave, the bold, the beautiful. You are the story I was
always meant to find.

Thank you—for your words that heal, for your hearts
that hold, for your voices that rise like an unstoppable
anthem.

The future is waiting— our poems yet unwritten,
our dreams yet undared. Together, we'll keep making
magic, turning paper into possibility, and shaping a
world where every voice matters.

This city sings me home. And for that, I am endlessly
grateful.

Cityquake

I run
and the streets split under my feet
like paper in a careless hand.
Neon scratches my eyes
and I laugh
because someone has to
and it might as well be me.
Walls lean in
but I lean back harder
leaving marks
like signatures no one asked for.
The city hums,
traffic blares,
sirens wail—
I dance between them
as if gravity
is as optional
as red lights
in St. Louis.
I kick doors open
I punch glass
I steal a look at the world
and grin—
because chaos is mine
to give away.
Hands in pockets,
jacket catching wind,

heart in riot mode—
I am fire in daylight
and the people watch,
and they notice,
and they step aside.
No apologies.
No plan.
Just streets shaking
under the weight of my laughter,
my mess,
my rebellion
alive
and untamed.

The Brightest One in the Room

She enters like she's already been applauded.
Like the spotlight is late,
and we're rude for not noticing
the art of her arrival.
Every word she speaks
drips with rehearsal —
a curated mess,
all lowercase vulnerability,
like a girl who's trying
not to be liked
but checks every mirror anyway.

She says she isn't jealous.
She says this often.
Which is how I know she is.
Jealousy has a smell.
Metallic.
Like bitten tongues and cold spoons.
It lives in the corners of compliments
that don't quite land.

She claps when I read
but not with her whole hands.
The sound is hollow —
a slow echo that never quite reaches the back row.
She says things like,
"We're all just doing our best,"

when what she means is,
"You're doing too well."

I watch her measure me
through side-glances and forced generosity,
her eyes tallying things she thinks I didn't earn —
the roles, the pages,
the man who looks at me
like I am already a legend.

She wants to be the smartest person in the room.
Wants to own the room.
Wants to be the room.
But rooms don't write.
They echo.
And I've never been interested
in reverberating someone else's noise.

Here's what she'll never say aloud:
She can't breathe in my presence.
Not because I take the air,
but because I make her aware
of how much she's faking it.

She wants to know how I do it —
how I make heartbreak into hunger,
turn silence into symphony.
But all she knows is the performance of pain.
She doesn't write for truth.
She writes for applause.

So let her collect followers like trophies.
Let her spit glitter and self-pity.
Let her stand beneath her own spotlight
and wonder
why no one is clapping anymore.

Because I don't need the stage.
I am the fucking poem.
And she's just someone who once tried
to edit me into something less threatening.

Love in the Lou (Swipe Left)

Dating here is like karaoke in a dive bar—
everyone swears they're good at it,
and everyone is lying.

The apps?
Mostly ghosts in Cardinals hats,
men who type like they're allergic to vowels,
and women who promise they're "poly"
but mean "I want to deceive politely."

Half of St. Louis is "ENM"—
which apparently stands for
Egomaniacs Needing More.
More attention.
More drama.
More people to disappoint.

They're hot one day, cold the next—
like the weather,
but with worse apologies.
They'll buy you a drink,
quote Bukowski badly,
and vanish before you finish your fries.

The gossip is louder than the music scene.
Screenshots passed around like communion wafers:
"Can you believe he said this?"

"Can you believe she matched with me too?"
Whole relationships die in Messenger threads
before they ever get to a first kiss.

And jealousy here has teeth.
Smile too long at someone else's maybe-lover
and you'll get branded a threat,
a thief,
a homewrecker
in a home that was never built.

I've seen less drama in middle school lunchrooms.
At least back then the pizza was a square that made
no claims of being beyond compare
and no one pretended to be enlightened
while throwing tantrums over attention
or shade over every new light's flare.

But still—
I try.
Because sometimes,
between the flakes and the fakes,
you catch a glimpse of something real.
A laugh that doesn't feel rehearsed,
a hand that feels like home,
a night that doesn't end in silence.

And maybe that's enough—
to keep swiping through the mess,
because sometimes hope
is just another bad habit.

Infinity River

The Mississippi doesn't care
if you call it beautiful.
It swallows what it wants—
barges, bottles, bodies—
and keeps on moving,
mud-thick and stubborn,
a muscle that never unclenches.
I stand on its edge sometimes,
watching it drag secrets downstream,
wondering which ones are mine.
It smells of rust and rain,
like an old, weeping wound
no one bothers to stitch shut.
This city pretends to tame it—
bridges stretching like handcuffs,
levees pressed tight against its ribs.
But water always remembers
where it's been,
and sooner or later
it comes back for what it lost.
I think of my mother,
her tides of vodka and silence,
how she drowned on dry land
while the river outside her window
kept rolling on, indifferent.
I think of myself,
how I've carried grief like driftwood,

how I've floated,
sputtered,
sunk,
and somehow surfaced again.
The river and I—we know each other.
We don't stop.
We don't forgive.
We carry everything,
and we don't let go.
But sometimes,
when the sun hits just right,
the whole muddy mess
flashes gold.
And for a moment,
you could almost believe
in redemption.

Hidden Corners

There are streets the maps ignore,
alleys that smell like fried onions and rain,
brick walls scrawled with murals
no one bothers to caption.
A dive bar with flickering neon
where the jukebox knows more secrets than you do,
and the bartender remembers everyone
but pretends she doesn't.
Sidewalks cracked just enough
to trip a tourist
but perfect for someone who's learned to watch their
    step.
Corner stores that sell nothing but cigarettes, chips,
and the soft promise of gossip.
A stray cat weaving between tables,
like it's the mayor of forgotten things.
You can find poetry here
in the way the light hits graffiti,
in the scuff of worn wooden floors,
in the smell of rain on brick
that no one else notices.
This city softly purrs
in corners where no one asks your name,
where you can vanish for a while,
or show up and feel entirely seen,
depending on how much truth you can stand to see.

The city hums quietly here,
but only for the brave—or the foolish.
These corners don't forgive,
don't comfort,
and certainly won't save you.
They will, however,
show you exactly what you are.

Corners like these don't shelter.
They sharpen.
They teach you to fight,
to vanish, to rise,
to notice everything
while pretending nothing matters.

Ashes and Alleys

I have carried ghosts down city streets,
their elbows digging into my ribs,
their whispers hollowing out my lungs.
I have slept with regret for company,
let it curl around me like smoke,
and woken to find it still there.
Smiling. Patient.
I have been loved, poorly,
betrayed, quietly,
and watched the world shrug
like it had nothing to do with me.
I have been a mirror to other people's fears,
and broken glass always cuts both ways.
I do not apologize
for the fire in my chest,
the hunger in my hands,
the way I take up space
and refuse to fold into corners
where the timid hide.
I will claw my own name
onto walls that never held me,
stitch my own wounds
with words that taste like iron,
drink the bitterness
you call poison
like it's ambrosia.
I have survived unnamable storms,

walked through alleys
that smelled like old blood and hope,
and kept breathing anyway.
I am not safe.
I am not soft.
I am not your warning.
Not your lesson.
Not your cure.
I return
when the night has claimed everyone else,
to stand among the wreckage and laugh.
Because survival is not enough.
I will not just live.
I will haunt.
I will rise.
I will burn.

Heat & Hum

The air sticks to your skin like a secret.
Humidity folds you into itself,
pressing sweat and asphalt,
beer and regret
against your chest.
Rain comes like a threat,
soft at first, then brutal,
washing graffiti into the gutters,
turning streets into rivers of memory.
The sun bangs down without apology,
spilling gold on cracked sidewalks
while neon signs flicker like tired eyes.
And somewhere between storms and sun,
you catch the city holding its breath,
waiting for you to notice
how wild it really is,
how it shapes you
even when you're looking away.

City of Small Stars

The Delmar star walk glints underfoot.
You won't mistake it for Hollywood.
These stars are quieter, humbler,
some nearly forgotten,
their shine swallowed by the pulse of the city.

Light pollution hangs like a curtain,
dimming brilliance,
but not enough to erase the sparkle entirely.
If you lift your head at the right moment,
you catch one, maybe two,
a wink from the universe
that says, "We see you."

People here talk about leaving.
They dream of New York, Chicago, LA—
streets where the stars are brighter,
where their own flicker won't feel so desperate.
They say, "That's where I belong,"
and yet they stay.

Because a big fish in a small pond
shines differently than a small fish
in an ocean of giants.
Your meager star—modest, stubborn, stubbornly
    alive—
would vanish in the glare of another city.

Here, it can flare without apology.
Here, it matters.

St. Louis is the gateway it claims to be,
but gateways are funny things:
they tempt you with promise,
with movement,
with escape,
and yet they keep you tethered
to the corners,
the alleys,
the small streets where your own constellation
still waits to be noticed.

Arch, a city of rivals,
of bruised egos and bright ideas,
of love lost and made
in the space between stars.
It hums quietly,
like it knows the truth:
that you can want more,
dream bigger,
and still belong here.

Sometimes, small stars are enough.
Sometimes, they burn too bright to be ignored.
Sometimes, the light is all that matters.
It need not guide, need not fill the cracks,
need not perform for anyone else's eyes.
It need only exist. Yours.

A pulse in the dark that belongs to no one but you.
A quiet flash that lingers long after you've gone—
scattered, dispersed, dissolved.
No longer a star, perhaps.
But once—once—you burned.

Denmark Laine

Denmark Laine is a poet, novelist and music critic who lives in St. Louis (but isn't too happy about it). He's been published by Spartan Press, STL TV Live, St. Louis Poetry Slam, *Panoply Zine, Sentience Literary Journal, Book of Matches, Another Chicago Magazine* and other cool places like that. He has a BFA in something from Southern Illinois University Edwardsville; maybe creative writing (mostly creative, not so much writing). He's the author of *Silversexuals, The American Paranoid Society, Thorazine Ice Cream Parlor, Immaculate Jones & the Love Pirates* and *The Martyr of Bughouse Square.* He's sometimes the art director for Back of the Class Press.

Ex Libris

I wanted to write my name
in the center of your labyrinth.

My minotaur is not seduced.
It is not aimless.
It has always known the way out.

It cannot be imprisoned,
only distracted.

In the maze we call "knowledge"
your little gold thread can lead you
only where you've been before.

A Postscript From Past Lives

for Alex

First
you were an iron torc around a Druid's neck
murdered in the barleycorn by three wisemen

drunk on the harvest; bard to every stone circle
where dryads took body in oakhearts and
laid to rest under a fairy mound
where a Roman god sleeps with one eye open.

Before that
you were an ayahuasca plant
strangling the trunk of a banyan tree,
growing darker in the Amazon
until you were smoked by medicine women
in their quetzal feathers and tobacco leaf hats;
too fond of serpent-love and jaguar-men.

Then
you were a red bee in the mountains of Nepal,
your mad honey, a tear that fell from the sun,
stung Tantra monks sick on spiraling nebula,
mumbling nothing for days
with the answer to 'who makes the grass green'
hidden up their sleeve.

Next

you were Orlando Furioso's broken sword
embedded in a cliff in the Pyrenees
after your friend and rival went off to jihad
and half of you sulked on the dark side of the moon,
roaring so loud after her rejection
you kept the last century awake.

And

you were a letter without a return address
penned by quill and laudanum
to a prostitute in Whitechapel,
found in the grate by some wigged Tory,
sold for a pound of sugarcane on malaria-ridden ship
that would never see the New World.

But

on the fourth day comes the astrologer from his
    crumbling tower,
the Cave of Seven Sleepers, Bronson Caves,
throwing off his ten-gallon hats and robot helmets,
wearing the next five years before everyone else.

Cupboard Love

for Sara

"By Your Side" - CocoRosie

The eloquence of your fidelity is wasted
on such a blunt verb as one man.

He bent you over the longest day
of the shortest summer,
waist-deep in a gown of heather
flogged with sweat bees.
Fed you sourwood honey
until weak at the knees.

What's left?
Main Street redacted by grass?
Your growing belly, another empty storefront?

Where his relatives are stubborn as landmarks
(wildflowers over-trodden with modesty)

who thought the bluebird was flightless,

where your phone is an unanswered prayer.

He has no ambition that can't be housebroken.
No talk of miracles except in sports.
His predictable cock is your scratching post.

Sweet, pathetic mooncalf,
he's as squeamish at a spot of your blood

as you are afraid of any gap you can't replace

with the half measure that he is.

Did you think Dom Pérignon
collects in the knotholes?

A Tudor prince squats in the outdoor latrine?

There are no swans mating.
Just a guidebook to covered bridges
that aren't there anymore.

You wanted a man
part lumberjack,
part Edna St. Vincent Millay
who looks at you the way
the axe handle recognizes the sequoia.

Not Keats' *La Belle Dame* in platform heels,
not a mantis' bride in Donna Reed pearls,
a child of ghastly innocence
who sows her perennial in a barren field.

Your eyes, both mercenaries,
uncommitted as loaded dice,
loving men the way a soldier loves his rifle,
and revenge, all you live on, is the light that fades.

Every drink interrogates your intentions.
Every favor costs interest.
Empathy, your garrote.

May the oppression of your looks fade
like the name on the water tower.

May the honesty you fought into remission
make all your wants a bed of nails.

May your weapon become as dull as his comfort.

Orpheus/Tim Finnegan

Orpheus/Tim Finnegan,
the sad song that you are
is for those who couldn't write it.

Orpheus/Tim Finnegan,
no blue guitar plays itself.

Orpheus/Tim Finnegan,
every hangover
is to pass from death unto life.

Orpheus/Tim Finnegan,
I am also torn apart
by women I couldn't love.

Orpheus/Tim Finnegan,
everyone's tears won't wash you.

Orpheus/Tim Finnegan,
when will you love again?
No two clocks agree in Dublin.

Orpheus/Tim Finnegan,
I'm not sorry.
I don't do anything for sport.
My heart eats what it kills.

Orpheus/Tim Finnegan,
the underworld is
wherever she is not.
Sing to the one
always behind
your observant back.

Stoned & Dethroned

Midnight velveting the steps of my reason,
morningstar-sandaled up to my porch
where tomorrow gapes
a sunburst, openmouthed.

Sitting in my own shadow,
a landlocked boat waiting
for something more,
for the tug of an imminent sea.

I play my laptop like a Steinway
if only for a page or so.

One single thought,
a quiet meteor,
a shouting light I can't hear
insisting:

I don't want to sleep!
The night has me by the heart!

I make my bed.
Clean my room.
Prowling for a dustless spot.
A place out of time
where a bodhisattva sat.

Mining distractions for epiphany.
Tantalized by defeat.
Life is short.
Art is long.

Doubt becomes addictive
when every day seems like coincidence.

Routine protests in me
against stifling comfort that
I work hard to keep
and work hard to avoid.

Apologies To Bashō

(Word Association Test)

TIME:

sleeps nose to anus.

PRACTICE:

doesn't make perfect,

it makes permanent.

SEX:

I never go looking for me in other people

...anymore.

MUSIC:

the _____ is on the ______

PEACE:

means missing no piece.

GROWTH:

always feels like loss.

It is.

PAIN:

makes all poison my medicine.

DESIRE:

fear.

FEAR:

desire.

For Rachel

When I said you're the one
I meant no one outnumbers you.

When I told them I'm not too young
I meant seasons won't change my mind.

I thought the world would never last.
That a thousand doors couldn't keep us apart.

Maybe sex was the only way
I knew how to ask for forgiveness.

In you was I reborn
the man who couldn't make you happy.

Still I carry you,

a debt I can never repay,

a recklessness of stars.

To drift with your ever-changing
dark blue *shakti* that crashes against me
flooded with awe,
consumed by the unattainable,
by what refuses to be summarized.
To be owned by what cannot be owned.

We should have loved as day swallows day.

We should have been sung in unbroken nights.

Yet fear will never conquer me.

You already have.

Long Pork

We're either raw or cooked.

Flesh mortified by gas stove,
by fillet and Ginsu knife.
Pan-seared stigmata
that branded boys with maturity.
Now injuries without initiation
to punish our bodies' inherited weakness.

Double-shift endurance tests
cleaning out grease traps,
fingertips chewed by garbage disposals,
deep-fried fatigue browned as pots
crusted in the sink.

The white scar on my hand is not a boast.
It flatters me with violence.
A fleck of scalding canola
glanced off a wire skimmer
marks us inmates of economy.

In Papua New Guinea,
a bamboo spike under the foreskin.
And while I've never been forced to swallow
my own circumcision, we have our bloodletting.

I've felt self-pity for veal carved for two,
unrecognizable hoof, snout and tongue
in the meat grinder.

A menu is a premonition.
Once an honor to consume
your loved ones,
your adversaries,

a diet of people,
the savory contrast,
emotional umami.

Thyestes' sons dished up like Paschal lambs.
Mothers doting, "I could eat you up!"

I must have gotten my chops in the shank of the
    evening,
silver stuck to my teeth, the taste of you between
    my molars.
Parting sinews dissecting gristle, a ripe seam splits
    the ribcage clean,
cartilage from bone, digested in the belly of Paris
    with no one to blame.
We are the Escoffier of our own limitations:
chefs who please no one,
waiters who go un-tipped,
harangued by stimulants on upturned milk crates,
chain-sipping saké until the night blurs.

Peeling potatoes, shelling clams,
risking pufferfish with no technique,
thumb against the blade like our nanas.
Trident hands stab the cutting board,
sharpening ultimatums.

Spending wages on our messy, savage craving
to consume and be consumed
our next and last meal,
tender girls skewered like kebab.

Jared C. Lewis

Jared C. Lewis, a Black American Poet and Father who refuses to let the rhyme die, writes because he has to. His debut, *Quarantine Chronicles,* which was written March 2020, is but a sliver. His first full-length collection, *A Leannán* will be available some time this year. He has toured from the country from Cali to D.C. with a most notable feature at The New York Poerty Festival and The New Jersey Poetry Renaissance. His main focus now is staying present and regulated.

New Devils

If I

were a devil?

Souls?

I'd have several.

Worlds?

In pebbles.

Trust?

There are levels

of passion

you have yet to

let set you

ablaze.

Be so kind?

Free your mind.

Let me

behead you.

red all over

no edits
no filters
it's clear
      an inventory
      of what I have

           new visions
           crude pigments
           hue's missing

               everything's
               black and white

           an old phone
           a dark room
           a lack of light

      an inventory
      of what I have

   strangers in a
   dirty mirror
it's clear
no filters
no edits

Let Me Be

I am black.

I am brown.

I am disgruntled.

I am american.

I am Native.

I am displaced.

I am oppressed.

I am UNSTOPPABLE!

I have compassion.

I have love.

I have friends.

I have demons.

I have secrets.

I have feelings.

I have doubts.

I feel rage.

I feel deep.

I feel lost.

I feel hope.

I feel....okay.

I am Man.
I am Here.
I am Light.
Let me Free

I Am All.
I Am None.
I Am Human.
Let Me Be.

I Am God.
I Am Flawed.
I Am Human.

OPERATION: Console

Who said you had to play their game?

Or obey their rules?
You see? It's all an elaborate ploy.
Grown children and their toys.
Yes. The sandbox does have rules
but a man has his choices.
I'll be the non-compliant
loser because

who says we have to play their games

or obey their rules?
It's hard to call it entertainment
when everything is at stake.
They're looking for a big fool.
I don't find that beneficial.
I choose not to engage.
you can simply walk away
'cause you don't have to play their games
nor obey their rules.

They have their call to duty.
Be it Halo, be it Doom,
Death has always been handheld.
The subscription's been renewed.
They'll continue bending rules
until we break...

...but we're breaking loose

The BLAZER

My bouquet wrapped in roses.
Heralding, My Sun,
My smile reflects your shine.
Dazzling, You are
Not the answer to my problems
But your presence is a pleasure.
I wish my lips could tell ya
What my eyes sigh all the time.
Scooch a lil' bit closer.
You're far too far for comfort.
Alas, it is a gift
I get to orbit, Your Warmness,
My bouquet wrapped in roses.
Heralding. My Sun.
You simmer in my eyes.
My morning has come.

A Bug's Life

Oh, how small I am.
Flea-sized are my worries.
As I scurry 'cross the doormat
on the porch of my Lord,
Goddess, My Earth,
my comforter.
Adored.
My Interpreter
and more...

Prowess

Peering past
perfectly pretty
pink placid
peonies petals
posing passionately
preserving permanent peace,
probably peeves Persephone
in particular.

Perhaps posies
plainly perpetuate
pleasing poetries!
Penning pleasant pads
and prose
per se
playful plateaus
providing pearlike pupils
places to precariously

peek,

poke,

pry

and prod past

pitchforked passages,

proud and prepared to parade upon

the presumed paradoxical paradises

of unapologetic

and unparalleled

peace.

Peace.

Peace.

Prayer #002 (A Lover's Prayer)

The setting Sun
Takes with it
All your pain
And scatters it
Within the night.
May your slumber
Be unburdened.
Far as The East
Is from The West
Be your woes
From your heart.
Worry none.
Drift peacefully.
I'll see you on
the other side.

Existence?

Moments spanning a lifetime.
Blips amidst the expanse.
Chances to live expanded.
Blessed with all the seconds.
Somewhere in the billions.
How many will you have given

to love?

How many will you have given

in jest?
If we give the majority
of our moments
to fear

then what have we become?

Cierra Lowe

Cierra Lowe, born and raised in St. Louis, product of EMS, the archdiocese, and the restaurant industry. Graduated from Webster University in 2015 with a BA in philosophy and from UMSL in 2022 with her BSN. She's published two full-lengths collection of poetry, *The Horse and the Water* (2017) and *Darken Your Door* (2023, Back of the Class Press) and is currently working on her third. Mother, ER nurse, middle class jester.

Love Lost

Life turns her face toward me—this time, the barrel of
    a gun
asking me the only question that really matters—
    splintered into
a million wavering facets, a riddle in every language
that I don't know how to speak:

Who are you? Why
are you here? How badly
do you want to be?

I know so many words, it seems.
Yet they all evade me when I need them most.

I've learned all about vanishing
from some of my favorite people. I have
opened fire into the afternoon sky, demanding
their release. I have crawled towards it,
intent to rip open the fabric of time and drag them
all home.

But the sky does not relent. So neither have I.

I've been every kind of sick I know, but
it's the getting better that counts in the end. I've turned
every place there is to turn—heavily against myself
some years—only to end up at each dead end.
The drugs don't actually kill you, most days.
They just make you forget how to live. My will

is intrinsically serrated. What I want is never
what I actually want.

So then what
is a little more confusion, a little more grief—a knot
in my neck, perhaps, or a new twinge in my wrist
maybe—when I am already a mason jar filled with
the memories of better people who did not have
    the luck
to survive themselves as I did? Tell me, by what kind
of artifice—what law, what awful magic, what sleight
of hand—might loss eat
from me today?

Every wound in the earth I've peered inside
has taught me a new name for hurt, a new place
inside me which needed to be filled. So I have dug
endlessly in this life, nailbeds stained
with the dirt I refuse to join—my fingers
some nights mostly tombstones.

At the end of the day substance was always
a cruel god, who ruled deafly and without forgiveness.
It was a lonely way to worship. Prayers
were each returned as blackbirds dissected
before me, entrails forever revealing my every
sin and shortcoming. Still today, my mouth
fills with feathers each time I must ask
for something that I need.
All pain is reproducible
I say, forever breeding
greater and greater lines

of succession. It is relief
that is often difficult
to come by.

There are so many ways in which
the body will ask for the things we can't—lips
turning blue to beg for breath, hearts speeding up
to spill the blood they cannot find to hold—but I
do none of these things instead. I spend most nights
awake in my most dedicated study of what is wrong
with others—and in the morning, the white lines
of the highway drag me back home. I am clean
in the way of an instrument which has been
    sterilized
after many gruesome uses. I long ago buried
the person I was when I was learning to survive, but
I'll still bring flowers to her grave on occasion.
Every graveyard on Gravois knows my name,
but has finally stopped waiting for me
to return their calls.

I, too, once wrote love letters
to drunk drivers and falling pianos. The guardian angels
of gas station tap water carried me across four state lines
just to drop me off at Kingshighway and Chippewa.
I've been demon gossip. I've lost entire years
to breaking.

And yet.

Today, I choose not to take stock of myself
by accounting for the things which are missing.

Secrets demand space inside of the body—I hide
    this one
in my stomach, like something which I must digest
endlessly. Like something I crave,
but can never taste.

Carbon steel overwhelms my palate.
Life—forever on her own terms—demands
her answers at last.

I tell her that I would flood Basin Street in brass
for a soul like this one—gifting back the heart
which I've been holding onto for a friend—shaking
and shimmying my way through the French Quarter,
busking the electric violin for one last
kiss.

I tell her that I do not know the word for this
    bloody crusade
in which I eternally war to stay where I am, but
that it will always be one of the things
I know best.

I tell her that she'll never catch me
with clean hands.

Appeased, she grants me
another day.

The Steeple

We all want the devil to save us
in the way he does, by taking
blame. I myself wouldn't be
so quick to speak ill of one
who has shown so much grace
in accepting guilt, however—even
if he has half the work ethic some books claim,
I've shared air with people who worked
twice as hard.

So I keep my head down
when I need to. I make calendars out of
string and Venn diagrams about
wristwatches and guns.

Every weapon holds some redemptive
benefit, you see, and every salvation poses
its own equal risk. Any blade can tell you
it is less lethal than
the clock.

The knife, for example—an instrument crated
to sever—can also be used to enter. To
visualize damage and repair it. I relieve living
tissue of dead. I cauterize every bleed
I find.

The needle—something used to suture, to
mend—can also be used to puncture, to instill.
I sew foreign coins into the linings of my coats.
I mark strange words into my skin.

One day, I'm going to invent
a reconstructive operation which creates
a new organ for holding memory. One day,
each of my most honest pleas will all be
re-discovered—now feral and fully grown—
within the haunted homes in which they
were born. One day, I'm going
to be harder than the shit
life keeps finding
to hit me with.

Loneliness is a strange, piercing note
which reverberates inside of the body—tonight
a velodrome of instincts gone awry—drawing
you into ever-deepening places. You don't know
how to swim, but you still listen for the ocean
in every shell you find. Salt burns
in every wound.

How many times
have I heard the words, "Please
help me," only to respond: "You're
going to be okay"? How many different ways
can a person say "It hurts"?

How many different ways
can I say "I know,
I'm sorry"?

Listen:

You are going
to be okay.

It hurts.

I know.

I'm sorry.

Julia Set

The only worlds I've ever learned to live in
were all given to me by people who were just
doing their best to get by. Every tongue in which
I'm fluent was taught to me by someone
who didn't know how to speak
honestly.

Every word demands an autopsy,
every glance a question. I swallow
my silence and it tastes like gold.
In Spanish my name is a command form
of the verb, "to close, to shut." In braille
my vertebrae read "have mercy." I write
odes better than sonnets. The Julia set
makes me cry.

Life is a strange magic that often ends
in vanishing. Like they say, every firearm
has a safety. So we must aim
to do better. I am determined
to discover a point of entry
which doesn't create
new wounds.

I await healing
to once again visit me
with miracles like balloons that will

be there for me to wake up to
tomorrow. But I know enough
to know better, so I keep myself
occupied. I teach myself how to
hardwire light fixtures. I listen
to the same song for eleven days
in a row. I drive alone at night. I fold
cooling hands and wonder
what the most incredible thing
they ever did was.

My hands—pruned
and blistered as they are—are always
making better and better mistakes
than yesterday. I withdraw,
remembering what I've said
about remembering.

Every intersection crosses with nostalgia.
Every apartment complex is an old number
whose door will not open for me anymore.
Every neon sign a good story,
every cemetery a reunion.

What is the opposite of a haunting?
Where does life end? When the spotted, arthritic
fingers of pestilence rob me of breath, I recall each
    time
I've survived without something seemingly vital
and figure, "What's one more?"

The darkness moans out my name, calling out for me
to let it wear me even thinner. You jaw thrust our
     union
again and again, begging with and in the only tongue
     we
both know to cease in its endless varieties
of obstruction. Your fingers ache
like my sternum must. But
there is no language I will not learn
to tell someone that
I love them.

Scene Six: March to the Sea

An eleven-year-old girl
crying about how a tree
grows around a fence, a whale
who sings at fifty-two
hertz: a reliquary
of adaptation, but also
absence.

Bells can only ring
because they are otherwise empty. I am
one hundred unsent letters, the black dog
haunting St. Roch's, the Mariana Trench
of women.

Life persists in darkness,
in heaviness, in silence—like agony
and like truth—yet reproach remains
forever shaped like two hands
wrapped around my throat.

We all architect the labyrinths
which occupy us yet—the perfect wound,
an ever-hollowing of each reiteration:
some days a plea for forgiveness, others
a demand for blood.

Tell me: what god
asks for this offering?
What altar holds it
without burning?

Mark of Cain

Life slips into my room at night
when I'm finally sleeping, sits
at the foot of my bed, and considers
me. She tilts her head to listen
to me—somewhere, still pleading
my case.

She is forever weighing my fate, each
moment a grain of rice in her scales.
She seemed to enjoy my labor, and so
I went to work. She seemed to enjoy
deploying my people to her severed
garden, and so I learned to tend soil.
She speaks to me in thousands of
beautiful and horrible languages,
some dead and some profane, and so
I learned the subtleties of dialect and
semantics.

She fancies her entry wounds as stars
she says, creating constellations which
tell the story of why I needed to allow her
to rearrange my vertebrae into a spiral
staircase and construct in me a fifth
chamber. And so I learned to read
the zodiac and stop bleeds. I've learned
to live with some scars. I'm always learning
new things for her.

She's forever inventing
new weapons to wield against me—you
being the most recent in a long and
formidable line—but I insist on charming
her into allowing me to persist.

I know, deep down, she
loves me. But not as much
as I love her, I suspect.
And so I had to learn
humility to stay—which
carries me further
than courage, and better
equips me to survive.

Life, forever searching for me to find lessons
worth keeping, falls back for me at last.
And once again, I dream
of nothing.

After Babel

All this love
was not gifted to me
by a jealous god.
To name yours is to
kneel before them. Instead I
call everyone I meet
an angel, and pick gravel
from my knees each night
before I go to bed
alone.

Nothing I know
has arrived intact.
Forever searching for the depth
of damage, uncertain of how
to stop triaging needs—I know
what it means to want
what breaks.

To recognize the moment a person
splits. How pain announces itself
before language. I see fractures,
and know how much to handle them.
I see the eye unwilling to be met,
the jaw that tightens instead of
speaking. I know what a person
can forgive, and what they
haven't.

I learned early
that survival wears
many costumes. I do not
stand to beg, but the languages
were broken long before
me. I do not confuse hunger
with faith. I do not lie, steal,
cheat or borrow. The devil
says please, so I don't
have to.

Grace finds me
in strange places now.
They call knowledge
power, but it doesn't serve
me. They call safety paramount,
but it smothers. They call restraint
strength, but it limps.

One eye sold, the other
shut—every rib
a wishbone.

Not everything lost
is gone. Even the ocean
coughs up the bodies
she's finished holding—we
all wish for home, you see?

Hearts held collateral
for wisdom murmur
all the same. I've heard
how silence can answer
prayers. I've seen miracles
no one asked for.

Jim McGowin

Jim McGowin prefers to create art when he isn't stuck at his day job. He dabbles in painting, video, graphic art, experimental music and writing. He is the author of several chapbooks and *Murmuration,* a book of poems published in 2018 by Spartan Press. He resides with his family and two cats in St. Louis MO.

A Slender Rod Used by Conjurers

The unseen scourge's press is devious, its heft
accreases dominance until prior affiance contorts in
odd angles just to keep the ciphers asleep.

To sate the coombing wae serene, a deed betide of
scission skin. To plait another's skein divined, fetch
hoary mollusk's pitch-lorn cast from deepest ocean-
cursed blind eye, and impersonate the motion versed.

Espying in spiral worded, a feint shift begets the page
edge torn - unto this will imperfect wile be thrifted
into incants sworn. A fie cry sieves, sounding twixt
arrowslits obscured by an inkhorn curtain. Uncertain
fate dims and duly follows, swiftly sly.

The depraver wand rouses nigh, a volley outspoken
- ousting cursed darts. The sniper gesticulates with
harmful secrets notched and riddled very sharp.

Tricky strafing wiles, cloven to a waning wound,
spattering designs surging from the all-too-familiar
hole. The grim-hewn soul yields - weeping abstract
works puddling to gild the floor in a ponderous
jitter, copious and amoebic, and slick with bitter
implications.

Even the Clouds Fear Clouds

Go quietly to the rainy places.
Faintly rift, swift the withering fire races.
Dimming the burning pangs of consciousness,
with far too many dancers in its slinking wisp.

All the fearful tangle swarms in, sins
deceptive love in the high notes,
writhing a ribbon to riddance.
Red layers of feeling slide and peel,
fluttered eyelids conceal guile,
while imprint dreams of unwondered
slip-ups slay, pilfered and unredeemed,
a blitz on bone on gone -
as brightness hesitates in non-existence.

Not everything will be revealed, ever.

Clever madness gathers
until it becomes a disguise.
Let us retreat within its ordeal,
until even the clouds fear clouds
and the beastly noises they conceal.

Go so quietly the very air breaks its scry -
the sound of sighing replaced by
the sound of begging replaced by
the sound of sobbing replaced by
the sound of a lightning-locked door,
painted the color of a faultless blue sky.

Egregore Agriculturalis

The storm front is never gentle counsel,
you will inevitably feel the grey burden of rain.
Roll over in your own bed and ignore it -
something heavier is already on its way.

The downpour woman is disfigured
by threshing appetites.
Her design is better than the pen
that drew her as a mere drizzling girl.
She owns the leaning trellis, intolerable
of garland grace, dumb with grasping,
groaning heavy and gnawed at gravely.

What dazzling sorrow fills wet hollows
with the sobbing sounds of parched grass,
last heard in the rumoring rasp's tell?
Take a harsh sickle to lush reason,
to sell a bitter bounty of questionable yield.

Your god is nothing but a feeling to feed.

Every starved season the neglected fields
are tilled, a history of clumped dirt and char.
The mud roots of words are wizened away.
Cracks in a stranger's tomb allow lively little lacings,
the grazers' mouths I have endured - a reminder -
despair is all I ever kissed with these green lips.

The price of deep ruts is obscured by the piled spilth —
tender seedlings ignored beneath an etiquette of brambles.
The ultimate structure of ploughing though fate
is a gamble of dowsing intersections.

Standing water is sometimes deeper than it looks,
but the ground can still drink it very, very quickly.

Mississippi Bladed

I won't say you wait for words but
I'll just sit back until
I go back
to backbones to board
a train rolling off a long-winded chorus.

Chased
not just up and down tree roots,
not just rusty water rushing round,
pretending to be steel,
spinning maddened wheels,
turn the conversation to blood splattered rocks,
reveal my dearth and pray the dirt covers it deep.

A man won't river, but he can sing a backwash
and a swallow on the heels of yet another year.
We've got this dream called taking a sleep.
We've got this caterwauling in the carousel.

I've got mine (take time),
I've got the time (take a breather),
I've got neither (take its toll)…

Happy to retaliate, happy to oblige,
swill the wish to apologize
for a beggar's pick and foolish hands.

Your choice groans from around the bend,
off the hitch, up turned stone,
spite these strange bones
pull like waded heels in mud,
yet the cities of ours go on rambling.

You stand your split ground,
unwilling to move. I don't know
what else to say…
Except I'll pretend to water you
with my dousing dream about fortune,
an expense the rain might wash away
in the unavoidable coming flood.

The Feinting Man

What a harsh old leech,
a worm wherein a light should hang
and burn candles in a dead goodbye gaze,
turning dreams to years and miles of taking.

A wall guides my left hand,
my right - blind touch -
the pale-eyed practice of simpering Galahad.
This discontented funeral needs work,
but there is something terribly tempting
in the reek.

I risk the gutter, the hand wound loathsome,
through which rain pours out to ruin
the wallpaper and the foundation,
mustering a creak in the Holy Grail faulds.

The feinting man is a mockery, insists
on acting anointed as a living legendarium.
The absolution given this black saint,
a knower of the contemptuous word "love",
is as unwise as a ceremonial sword.

There is metal enough to be hard within,
but I am disquieted by the dirt
cleansed away from the muted body.

It is regrettable and haphazardly heaped,
foreshadowing the places where the dead
have already dug convenient holes for each other,
from which they pretend to be born again -
chivalrous, unalloyed and tempered.

The Confetti People

We touch east, we preach west.

Heaven means one should stand still
and stay blind to pestilence.

Emptied of all his clothing, a man
is nothing but a hem.
Throats clear in the balcony.

We cut here. We splice there.
Gray decaying in the light, forever.

The big escape. The performative fiction.

And all over the floor, the unswept confetti grows.

August 2016

I can hear the night's
footsteps.

It is obviously wearing
heavy boots.

Fear of the coming wind -
that it will mess up my hair.

I look at my reflection
in a funeral parlor
urinal.

Dandelion Flames

Years have passed while
I spoke to the thinness in the dark,
split like a lip, grinding teeth
as the bell country tolls.

Your pale voice tatters in a frail cloth
tangled in a spindly branch -
or maybe it's a snake's shed skin,
or a love canal promise of salvation.

Habitually divided,
you claim like a church, vindicated
with the sort of illumination
that can easily be turned off with a switch.
Behind you, always another dark
corner to turn.

Through colored glass
the sky is crushing with dandelion flames.
Our seeds are tossed, lost
behind in a survival trick,
veering violently, owned
only by a breeze.

The compass spins to aim you at your pain,
pointing in one cardinal direction.
The shoulders of the pall bearers are spokes
on a wheel spinning ever lower.

Our hearts will fall, eventually turning
to rewild space with what we forgot to finish.

I find myself rooted
in everything that is not you.
The fire has taken all,
but I did manage to plant a few good things,
there in the wastes where nothing
much will grow.

R. C. Patterson

RC Patterson, Ed.D., has been an adjunct lecturer in philosophy at Harris-Stowe State University for seven years. He has an M.A. in Philosophy and an M.Ed in Adult & Higher Education from the University of Missouri – St. Louis. He earned a Doctorate in Education in May 2024 from the University of Missouri – St. Louis. Dr. Patterson has been published in the Gasconade Review, Back of the Class Press, Black Noise and Bad Jacket. Dr. Patterson has seven published works of prose and poetry, including "You need to be tougher," "I ain't got it," and "Inside out" as part of an anthology by Back of the Class Press titled *Not Ready for River Styx*, the collection *Black Magic*, published through Spartan Press, *Deinósology, Elegies, The Necropolis of Abraxas, Act of Hericide, You Need to be Tougher, House of Ganesha, Lógica Básica y Psicoanalismo, La Maldición de los Inocentes, Introduction à la philosophie, Acuarelista, The voice of the father is a gunshot* and *Ideas.*

Welcome to church!

Welcome to church! All those perched on bar stools,
Drunk enough to bring a bathing suit to the car pool
I remember when I was just like you, quite rude
Drunk stumbling into open mics, crude
                as Picasso with his Lyndon Baines Johnson
painting portraits of my points in your mind with a
                        nail gun,
            automatic, a touch sensitive rail gun
                through your colorblind veils, run
        like Christmas lights strung across gutters in July
                decorating stale spider spun
    passage ways through webbed fantasies one must
            break through to sip the Holy Grail,
once tossed about on the white sail powered pail
                        horse,
            as she was taken to Apocalypse
            tortured with Darkside's rawhide whips
            erased Maninka, Fon and Arabic
She said that she didn't give money to homeless white
                        men
Because they could jaunt into her bookstore and Snap,
                whip crack, take it
    Hyperbole is the language of those annoyed by
                colorblind explanations.
            Images of white men entering the store
    laying claim to book, bookshelf and building,
            stating "My destiny manifests"
            Then along came a pail horse

Drunk stumbling, crude
as Picasso with his Lyndon Baines Johnson
painting portraits of its points in your mind

Floor mite

I dive Wright through road blocks, Doc Jones
swimming through slave cemeteries and various gory
historic trappings
In militaristic religious vestments RSF and SAF box,
bones
pile up. Sudanese famines, retaliatory kidnappings

Bedouins and Druze. Druze have a protector
That appears in bombs, fragments, but not in memory.
Where was the minority protector during the reign of
the prosector?
They were silent as the dictator to those he deprived
of sensory

experiences in nebulous known unknown
penitentiaries.
The backs of Fed vans where agents can disappear you
Some agents have. They gave them our voices, the
unrepentant sectaries.

But they didn't expect what they expected.
Paramilitaries! Yes! They still hear you
talking foolishly. They learned from your spite
The door is locked. Now they can crush your rancid
paradigm, you floor mite.

J'ai vu une vieille femme, sans maison

I drove by a homeless old lady. Car stopped at the
red light
A warning, she was adored in a wool coat, in
85-degree heat
Asking people for something, her need bled right
Through to my desire to appease, unfortunately feats

of kindness are outside my capacity. I lack the
elasticity
of luxury goods. Kindness is rhodium, the rarest
of the platinum family.
Hard to find, harder to keep. I remember my cousin
with brilliant chromaticity
Asking what I happened to be writing in the back
of church, my response was clammily

given, half assed. I felt as though I came off
patronizing
That was not my intent. I just felt that the content
was too stupid. And I couldn't
explain this thing I was revising, its aluminum I had
barely started anodizing

If that lady dies in street, I think I'm partly
responsible

Not as responsible as the dogs who man-slaughtered
my baby cousin and her baby.
Why shouldn't
we all be held responsible?

Laugh in schadenfreude

From - "Acuarelista"

High prices,
game console price hikes,
I laugh in schadenfreude
as I'm bleeding green
I overdosed on Hopium,
they see a carpenter screeding, "Preen
the feathers of government"
they think but with ICE strikes

Preen the feathers of the establishment
recalcitrance brought us to hard times
through space and time,
the new guard spimes
with neurolinks
furthering the national ravishment

Hope you learned your lesson, submitting to your
Heracles Idiots saying *do your research*
should have listened to Moerocles.
Idiots seated electorally
beneath the sword of Damacles

hearts emptied of hope
must weather this tragedy of Xenocles
Beyond tristes
and old forms of organization
You will survive this damnation

You vote for the clown you get the circus

From - "Acuarelista"

Programs cut, layoffs loom,
dental issues endemic
regret for an idea once rooted
like a fir, cus
out bozo boozed out
on conspiratorial polemics,
You vote for the clown
you get the circus

A carnival of Eric Andre impersonators
Pranking babies birthed in PFAS,
anti-intellectual
wannabes sipping piss
from rich urinators
blame fornicators
for the fall of the west, ineffectual

Idiots ignoring the systemic,
preaching
noncompliance to consistency
from corporate corpses
of high horses
thinking they are reaching

Beyond death to golden hamlets, heavenly
thorpses
to eternity and blessedness
of affordable groceries
Actually,
chose suicide and poverty's coteries.

Spinal fluid

Death chants, creep up the back
Firey Red ants,
a venomous lumbar puncture
Ruptured bone,
damage,
spinal fluid dynamics
studied critically by fiesta masks masking

Refugees starving, sour, dough needed in
Rising temperatures
Melting flesh from bone,
the displaced dissolving digesting themselves

Crack a canine,
pull pins,
rip rivets from rubble,
fight tooth and nail,
trapped in the troubles

Exploratory Surgery

He asked his cousin:

"Where is your car?"

The cousin sighed and replied,

"At the mechanic."

Since he took his car to the mechanic, he thought his
fears would be over. His fear still exists, but he masked
it up. Bandaged un cut skin. Disguised a lie. This
morning, he took his ailing progeny to the hospital.
The father and mother were unable to resolve the
problem.

The mother thought, "Maybe he has a virus?"

The father replied, "Maybe?"

The doctor said,

"I don't know what the problem is, but I can examine
it with an exploratory surgery. Let's remove each
organ and see what happens. If we think the organ
is necessary, we'll place it back in the body. There are
actually a lot of organs in the body. Some of which are
completely useless!"

With the doctor's confidence, the parents left.

While operating the familial automobile, the father saw the check engine light. Now, on the precipice of some acute psychological break down, the couple took the car to the mechanic.

Now careening over the edge nearly into the shadow of the valley of suicidal despair the mechanic told them:

"I don't know what the problem is, but I can examine it with an exploratory diagnostic procedure. Let's remove a part and see what happens. If we think the part was necessary, I'll put it back in the car. A car is actually made up of many parts."

El Amor que Arde

From - "Acuarelista" (Con un cambio. ¿Puedes encontrarlo?)

Sus ojos pueden ver mis deseos,
a través de las tormentas, parecemos
differentes, pero sonamos igual - nos damos besos
cantamos en armonía. Establecemos

algo nuevo cada vez que hablamos
sobre su dolor, de sus esperanzas.
Construimos un hogar y fablamos
de historias nacidas en la desesperanza.

¿Cuánto tiempo puede durar?
Tiempo está suspendido, una fruta
cuelga. Ellos saben que asegurar

que nuestro amor es profundo, una gruta.
Es eterno, en este invierno
eterno. Nuestro amor arde, un infierno

Femme du Combat

From - "Acuarelista"

Les bâtiments en pierre, les fleurs
mourantes sur des étagères aussi hautes
que des tours. Souviens-toi de l'heure
Il est né de l'éternité par sautes!

La peau brune de mes mains s'assèche.
Oshun a émergé des rivières bleues
Abèbè, sensualité est plus fort. *La fleche!*
J'ai vu les livres sacrés, o Morbleues

qui chante les louanges des Noirs,
parler contre l'Africain - blasphème
c'était écrit dans le grimoire.

Le paroissien dit: le curé est le graphème
qui prescrit le baptême. Pour
nous, elle bat ce monde de vautours!

Return of the Letter

From - The voice of the father is a gunshot

The letter always
returned to the signified
The Mother!
That cruel un dignified
minister dementia
daily stole her letter
From beneath
the gaze of the king,
a rage festered
In the hearts
of the court guards
and timid eyes
Of all who
witnessed the cries,
incoherent
Utterances until three women devised a mission,
like Charlie's Angels,
ripping through the darkness, straight through
The palace apertures,
the arched,
weak gate ways, to
Take this great queen
to a safe place, who
Are you?
She asked repeatedly,
until Dupin

Returned the letter,
now she could see
these beings
of ethereal beauty.
So, it's true that
The letter returned
to its foundation

Sadly, this is not
true in all cases.

Brett Underwood

Brett Lars Underwood is a St. Louis poet and promoter of happenings and mishaps. He has the wingspan of an albatross and favors the brushback pitch to preemptive warfare. He is the author of *MUSH* (Spartan Press, 2018), *MUSHARONA* (Kung Fu Treachery Press, 2020) and *GATEWAY TO MUSH* (Spartan Press, 2024) as well as a couple chapbooks and various journalistic endeavors.

Yippy Didn't Do It

No never mind yells at corresponding dick
move pours fruit juice into half a glass
of malt liquor queen screams
witness to the contents
of the sausage.

Just sayin'.

The beer gods cry under the glow of ferris wheels
dating the paradise
because of some lighting weirdness
pair of dice rolled.

The potholes smile with little puddles of blood
and axle grease edible video streams
of a nation down the drain
but the world is more than little thoughts
until you are dragged off by fascists.

Mud Shoes

It rained
Still
You had to walk
on a Tuesday morning
on a Wednesday night
like a lost sailor
with no sea
no waves to bob on
no boat to set sail
Still
a destination was set
one step
starts it all
Slippin' probable.

Say It Like John Wayne

If it gives you wood
"Revise and reframe the potential,
Pilgrim."

Would that they had SPERMICIDE.
                The Pilgrims.
That would solve this traffic problem.

You hate dithering!
Leonard Cohen emitted from Iggy Pop
                Oh! Get off it!
There is a vehicle called a segue
                This world is not all about you.

This
    is not about me.
Words are
            not about you.

Shhhhhhhhhh.
Chew silently.
Get a drink.
Take a puff
Make peace with yourself.
Breathe.

The sun clouds...
and then there is a pigeon waiting for death.
There are two men stuck on a sidewalk
exhaling plumes of smoke.

Walk outside.

Walk into the dark.

Dare.

Like the frog leaping under
a lily pad
less than a mile away.

Hollow Machismo Insecurity

Dulcimers pair well with mushroom gravy
    decalcomania.
Their notes don't bother to follow the outlines,
but play to their color.

Stuff your hollow machismo insecurity
with their essence.
Form it into a stick
and smear it on your resting
bitchface.

The Front Porch

It is my cosmos
Some days
These days
Of Nothingness in
Between jobs
As a man bicycles by
West on Alberta

I still remember those
People
Those loves
Those friends
Those strangers
And artists
Poets
Under a giant tree

But now, walking
Up Gustine
I see even larger trees
And more strangers
Turn around.
Return home
To the porch

As the trash truck clunks
In the back alley

A forlorn soul
Sits in there and works
The levers
Taking away
The unwanted.

For now
There is beer
and eggs
rice and beans.

Writhe Arises

Hurting Twister, you're a little out of sorts right now,
so try to slow down footstool strut withering awaits
fluttered rethinking and take life
furthering satiated twinkle at the romorrow pace
though you'd prefer tomorrow.

It's one of those Phoozetool truest
writhing days when you need to explore
each mood as it trusting writhe arises
and get to the shutting writer bottom of it all.

Romorrow? When is romorrow?

City Rules

We had a place on the South Side.
Grey windows took the art of sunshine
out of the equation, but there was the music
of the street.

Bunnies were at play out back
when the pups weren't too exuberant,
but when they grew to be snarling
alarms to the activities happening next door
in light and dark.
No play for the bun buns.

...and if you didn't rest
the passenger side wheels
up on the curb,
upon arriving home
from a long day of toil
and trouble
you might be missing
a side panel in the morning.

The city has its own rules.

Ear plugs, white noise
allowed sleep to some
in other more gentle
parts of town,

but it was cans of corporate lager
that brought slumber in our world.

Ignoring the possible need for tuck pointing,
we managed to pay the bills
underneath hovering helicopters.

The places are now within an easy walk
to all kinds of delicious food,
even though the squirrels
devoured the old garden

Quietest Inbreeding Salon

In the aborted stoic twilight
get artistic with blood

               Help locating a salesman
biologist call detraction tablets
with battles growth idiotic
looking for deer antlers
               It's the best way
We have no better way

Questionable ingredients
in the aborted stoic twilight
questionable ingredients
deliberating on quietness

Arm was found by a stranger
turned out vital to set up
alternative income
bandwagon farm elitist
treasury watchdog

Nosebleeds quieting train
in the stoic twilight
deliberating on quiescence.

Rest The Pest

It's a great time for an ending
great and great and time ending
strange nightmares.
Break off that toxic relationship
and do it so for the cowboy segment.
Space is surreal enough
and multiple versions of y'all
in the sunbread (or sun bread?)
as usual.

Finish that colossal project and Swedish no?
Or just try quitting or quilting that bad habit
one more time and ending great and great
and time ending.

You can do it, and it's for the best time
or rest the pest and do and do and don't
stop squinting shine whine cut.
MmmmK?

Bus Stop Logic

Another skit(ter brain) idea:
Long, braided dirty-blonde hair
of a diminutive woman
in the self-checkout lines
interactions otherwise
puzzling
to most consumers.
                    Or are they tools on a search?
What?
                          The tools. The braids.
I know but, what?

Exactly! And exchange the "t" for a "y" and you don't
   have "but", but "buy"!
That's what's happening, but there it is again: "but".

Even the gadgets seemed puzzled
as all poke at them
in attempts
at escape.
Why are we here? It would be disturbing to do the
   math.
                       Where are you "in
there", Rapunzel,
equally displaced and shrill.
Sensing that no one is gonna climb
Any

time

sooon.

I'd like to chop up some vegetables and add them
    to your ramen,
But, uh, hey,

            even I don't have any cash…

AND I AM NOT EVEN IN THIS
    SUPERMARKET.

    I read about you in a 'zine.
                AND REMEMBER?
Pine Tree State Mind Control talking about the
    first words you see upon entering?::::
PRODUCE!
C'mon, ROOKIE! Get at it!

            I gotta get the fuck outta here.
CUT!!!

Daniel W. Wright

Daniel W. Wright is a poet, editor, and fiction writer. Wright is the author of five full-length collections of poetry, six poetry chapbooks, two novels, a short story collection, and co-author of four poetry splits. His work has appeared in numerous print and online journals including *Chiron Review, Book of Matches,* and *Gasconade Review.* Wright currently resides in St. Louis, MO where you can usually find him in a bar or a bookstore.

How Many Raptures is That Now

From Y2K to the Mayan Calendar,
they've been predicting our end
for as long as I can remember.
And when the fast kill doesn't follow through,
we're stuck with the slow suicide.

And those who prophesize
the end of days
while making a tidy profit
preach about a lack of morality.
The rest of us just live
like anyone would—
with the world ending
any day now.

Like… for real…
Seriously…
any day now…
annnny day now…

There's always a reason
a day or two later
why the end never came.
And it's always the fault
of us sinners,
who were going to be left behind
when it came time to cash out
anyway.

A Brief Moment of Stardust

The snow falls
on the last day of November
as I put on a Willie Nelson record.
Night is beginning to fall
and soon I won't have a friend to talk to
about whatever thoughts
cabin fever can bring.

Like how I am middle-aged
and have no more money for rainy days
and soon I will not be a first round pick
for a job
as the world still thinks people my age
are gearing up for retirement
at 65 or 70.

No child, no partner, and no chance
for that in the hands that were dealt.
Not bitter,
but wish I could have been given.
half a chance to make ends meet
more than I was given

Outside the snow looks beautiful as it falls.
Inside my mind spirals
I keep such spirals
from the friends I talk to

because sharing them
will solve nothing.
While all this is going on,
I listen to my friends
and I feel better.
knowing I've made them feel better
That's enough to be
a momentary stardust
for me to make a wish on
and hope things will be better for all of us
on the other end
of the darkness we all brace for.

In the Land of Static

Under the glow of a fading moon,
a red curtain flickers, pulling me in—
voices speak in half-whispers
soft as velvet
while fingers brush the edge
of what we know.

A diner hums in midnight air,
plates clattering
like forgotten ashes
while the staff moved like memories
who remembered everything
but never told anyone.

Making love to the idea
of America providing the soundtrack,
to the soft underbelly of the jukebox,
where coffee tastes like nostalgia.
The highway curls,
swallowed by smoke,
where lost souls drift in the rearview,
their faces smeared with dust and longing.

Through the cracked screen of a television,
a dancer spins, adrift from time,
her eyes hollow,
her smile both alluring and foreboding

And behind it, something darker—
a scream drowned in love,
a laugh twisted by desire.

And though the dream dissolves at dawn,
we remain—
haunted by the shimmer of what could be
the poetry of silence
where the shadows wait
and the longing of what we cannot name.

Stick My Head in the Oven Like a
Good Poet Should

After finishing my set
sharing poems about my childhood,
a woman came up to me
to tell me
how much she enjoyed my set,
how heartfelt
she thought my poems were.

I thanked her.
Before I left,
she wondered
if she could ask
one more question.

I turned, smiled,
and said, "Sure."

"How have you never killed yourself?"

I didn't know how to respond.
The thought has crossed my mind —
especially when I was younger.

In the moment,
I wanted to say
that although it was difficult

I never wanted to give in
to the assholes
who made my life
a living hell growing up.

But something about her question
suggested she wanted
something more flowery.

I thought of telling her
that no matter how bad it got,
I always knew
life was worth living —
but I didn't want to lie.
Because there were times
I thought of dying
out of spite.

Dying
to not deal with insane bullshit
from people who wouldn't own up
to being wrong.

Dying
because nothing on this planet
seemed worth living for.

I thought of giving the reasons
I always found to live.
A funny story that could deflect.

Or maybe ask her
what it was about those poems
that made her ask that question.

But I didn't know
how to turn
an honest albeit weird question
into a therapy session.

So, with no other option,
I said,
"Just lucky I guess."

She smiled and left,
leaving me to nitpick
about her adoration —
how it was enough to get a compliment
but not enough
to buy a single book.

And leaving me
wondering
if she thought I was crazy
for giving her an answer
that even I wasn't sure about.

When No One's Looking

Healing isn't pretty
It isn't green smoothies
and live, laugh, love.
It's lonely as hell.
It's your mind tricking you
into false truths
that no one gives a shit.

It's wanting to be sexy to someone
even though that someone
may be the worst choice for you
and you know you have to break the cycle
where you can.

It's knowing that there will be
no congratulations
for doing the work
and not seeing the results
because a pot never boils
when you stare at it.

It's the reality
that you may outgrow a friendship
without telling someone
because you can only do so much
of the heavy lifting
and you only want them to keep up

if they're willing to keep up
on their own.

And maybe you won't feel better
for a long, long time—
but you'll know you didn't lie to yourself.
You did something.
You may want someone to notice.
Most won't.
Heal anyway.
Silence has its own kind of applause.

East of Spring

There is peace and beauty in a garden
as the seasons come and go,
but today is the first day of the year —
I'm east of Spring.

Taking advantage of the fact
no one called dibs today,
I'm free to play in the jungle gym of my mind,
for a moment too brief for me.

Sometimes I feel seventeen again,
listening to music I can feel deep,
writing whatever thoughts come
as I stare at the clouds.

Sometimes I feel like I'm ten,
riding a bike,
aiming for the steepest hill
just to catch the breeze —
catching the wind like a secret
only I could know.

The whole summer used to open up
like a dare.
Sticky popsicle lips,
the sharp sting of gravel in my knee,
the laugh I let out anyway.

Now summer feels like a photograph
left too long in the sun.
But here in this garden,
with the music low and the sky soft,
I catch a glimpse of it again.

I'm east of Spring,
pedaling forward,
half in memory,
half in now.

Diss Tracks

Like many a popcorn gif,
I lined up with everybody else.
to see two ego maniacal man children
battle it out over social media
like a couple of bratty teens.
Joining in a chorus of "ooo's," "aaaah's," and "no, he
    didn't!"
Reveling in the pettiness of two men
who I honestly hoped would just drop dead
to make the world a better place.
Do we ever leave high school?

Timing Was Never My Strong Suit

Funny, isn't it,
how timing can wear a different name
when it suits the story better.
You're ready now.
You're all in now.
And I'm not angry
just aching in the silence
of everything I was willing to be.

I don't want you back.
That's the part that's hardest to explain.
I don't miss the waiting,
the guessing,
the almost-love that never crossed the line.
But still—
it stings to watch you leap
when you barely took a step with me.

I hope they hold you gently,
the way I would have,
if only you'd asked.
I hope you build a life
out of all the things
you were too unsure to give me.
And I hope I heal
in the shadow
of your newfound certainty.

This project was made possible, in part, by generous support from the Osage Arts Community.

Osage Arts Community provides temporary time, space and support for the creation of new artistic works in a retreat format, serving creative people of all kinds — visual artists, composers, poets, fiction and nonfiction writers. Located on a 152-acre farm in an isolated rural mountainside setting in Central Missouri and bordered by ¾ of a mile of the Gasconade River, OAC provides residencies to those working alone, as well as welcoming collaborative teams, offering living space and workspace in a country environment to emerging and mid-career artists. For more information, visit us at www.osageac.org